Critic

"Yisroel is an accomplished artist, musician—and now, with this, his first book, an author. His words seek to inspire us—to paint thoughts on the canvas of our minds that dance with the energy of his music. May his words inspire us to reach heavenward with genuine passion and understanding."

~ Rabbi David Fohrman, author of *The Beast that Crouches at the Door* and *The Queen You Thought You Knew*

"Through heartfelt stories and meaningful parables, Yisroel empowers his readers to reach their unlimited potential. This inspiring book is written for anyone looking to deepen their relationship with G-d and themselves."

~ Aleeza Ben Shalom, the Marriage Minded Mentor, author of *Get Real, Get Married*

"The saying goes, 'Words that are said from the heart go strait into the heart.' Reb Yisroel's soft spoken easy to digest style complement his inspirational mesage, making this new book a work that has the capacity to speak to everybody—no matter where they are on their personal journey at the present moment."

~ Rabbi Eliyahu Yaakov, author of *Jewish by Choice* and *The Case for Judaism*

"Yisroel Juskowitz weaves together beautiful words of Torah, heartwarming stories and accounts of his own personal journey to present this heartfelt work on essential Jewish topics. His sweetness and authenticity shines through on every page."

~ Rabbi Shlomo Buxbaum, Executive Director of Aish of Greater Washington

Also by Yisroel Juskowitz:

Music: "The Narrow Bridge"
Art: Fine art, caligraphy, and micrography Judaica
Audio: "The Hidden Path" audio series

Coming soon: The Hidden Path Retreats!
For more information,
email: yisroel@yisroelworld.com.

For more information, visit
yisroelworld.com

The Hidden Path

An Extraordinary Journey
of the Mind, Body, and Soul

Yisroel Juskowitz

You have shown me the Path of Life,
In Your Presence the fullness of joy,
In Your right Hand, eternal bliss.

Psalm 116

KODESH PRESS

This book is dedicated to my dear parents and wife Kelly who have been supportive and encouraging in more ways than they can imagine. This book would have never happened if not for your help.

Thank G-d I have been blessed with so many special friends and family in my life. Many of them have helped with the chapter dedications, and their help has been immeasurable.

Here are the dedications:

FOREWORD: UNLEASH YOUR POTENTIAL: Dedicated by Fayge & Chaim Kasdan in honor of their children Miri, Ryzee & Frieda: May they each forever maximize their potential and achieve great heights!

CHAPTER 1: FINDING GOD EVERYWHERE (EVEN THE MOST UNLIKELY OF PLACES): Dedicated by Ari Weintraub in honor of his mentor, friend, and inspiration, R' Yanky Yarmish.

CHAPTER 2: REACHING OUT TO OTHERS: Dedicated by Shmuel and Ruchie Weinstock in honor of Ruchie's parents Yisroel Ephraim ben Shlomo Reuven and Yehudis bat Shmuel Moshe. They exemplify the kind act of giving. By watching them share and help others, they have become role models to their children.

CHAPTER 3: THE INNER LIGHT OF HASSIDUT: Dedicated by Eitan Katz to all of the Jewish People.

CHAPTER 4: PRAYER; TRANSFORMING OUR WORLD, TRANSFORMING OURSELVES: Dedicated by Nochi Krohn in honor of his dear wife Penina.

CHAPTER 5: FINDING THE LAND OF ISRAEL INSIDE OF US: Dedicated by Sue and Tova Kalkstein in loving memory of their father and grandfather Moshe Feivel ben Yosef Mordechai.

CHAPTER 6: LOOKING FOR LOVE IN ALL THE RIGHT PLACES: Dedicated by Aaron Ihnen in honor of the love of his life Chrissie Lynn Feit.

Chapter 7: Extending Your Hand: Dedicated by AJ and Diana Juskowicz in loving memory of Charles and Matla Schechter.

Chapter 8: Connecting Through Creativity: Dedicated by Anna Chana Iglanov in loving memory of her father Eliyahu ben Penina.

Chapter 9: The Beauty of Torah: Dedicated by my mother in loving memory of her father Nachum Leibowitz, whose love of Torah knew no bounds. He is an inspiration to me.

Chapter 10: A Deeper Look at Suffering: Dedicated by my father in loving memory of his parents Tzipporah and Alter Juskowitz, who were Survivors, but nevertheless built and raised a beautiful Jewish family. They are inspirations to me.

Chapter 11: The Gift of the Sabbath: Dedicated by Esti Strauss in honor of her dear friend Elisheva M. who has inspired her greatly, changed her world and gave her Esti's name.

Chapter 12: What it Means to be a Jew: Dedicated by Jon and Sima Greenstein in loving memory of Linda Danziger.

Chapter 13. Healthy Body, Healthy Soul: Dedicated by Julie Eisen in honor of her grandmother Ivy Eisen who has taught her how to be both healthy in body and spirit.

Chapter 14: Renewal and Redemption: Dedicated by Eric Feinstein in loving memory of his father Pinchas ben Yekusiel.

Afterword: Yearning for Godliness: Dedicated by Malka and David Flamholz in honor of their sweet children Baruch, Tali, and Nava.

Table of Contents

Foreword
Unleash Your Potential

Our deepest fear is not that we are inadequate. Our deepest fear is that we are powerful beyond measure. It is our light, not our darkness that most frightens us. We ask ourselves, who are we to be brilliant, gorgeous, talented and fabulous? Actually, who are you not to be? Your playing small doesn't serve the world. There is nothing enlightening about shrinking, so other people won't feel insecure around you.... As we let our light shine, we unconsciously give other people permission to do the same. As we are liberated from our own fear, our presence automatically liberates others.

~ Marianne Williamson

Ever since I was a little boy, I loved to dream. I was always the one daydreaming in class about all sorts of wild things. Inevitably, I would hear, "Yisroel, space in!" This would bring me sharply out of my fantasy land and into the reality of an entire class giggling and a very annoyed looking teacher. It reminds me of a joke from Stephen Wright, one of my favorite comedians growing up. He said he once got a postcard from his friend George. On it was a big satellite picture of planet Earth. On the back it said, "wish you were here." As a child, I dreamed of being a superhero. I, of course, had super powers; naturally I would be able to fly and had a long red cape (usually my bedroom blanket or the towel from the bathroom) to prove it. I would fly over the city using the dark of night as my cover I would rescue children from burning buildings, little old ladies who were being mugged, store owners who were being held up. The list went on and on.

As I grew older, the daydreams continued but the fantasies were different. Now I was an NBA basketball star. I would shoot baskets, lay-ups, three point shots, and slams, always with a little swish with the accompanying roar of the crowd. I would do a little nonchalant wave to the crowd; anything more would be losing my cool. Somehow, I was six-foot-eight, even though my Jewish genes certainly didn't say so. (A Jew may *own* a basketball team, but doesn't usually *play* on a basketball team.) So of course my Jewish mother talked some sanity into me.

Then I dreamed of becoming a famous artist. As a young child I used to doodle in class when I was bored. Later it grew to selling caricatures of the teachers during class (all fun, until I got caught). Then it continued with color war banners, to art contests, to pastels, and finally, to realistic oil painting. This was my dream, but thankfully, once again my Jewish mother, foreseeing a lifetime of poverty and food stamps, stepped in and saved the day. (They say the difference between a Jewish mother and a boa constrictor is that boa constrictors eventually let go.) I say this all only jokingly and lovingly, since I give full credit to my mother for keeping me on the ground and practical when I needed it the most.

As an imaginative person, I still day dream to this day. All of us do at times. When we stop dreaming, we stop being alive. The common denominator of my dreams was one goal; I yearned for greatness. I yearned to make a difference in the world.

But isn't this what we all yearn for at some point in our life? Don't we all want to reach our potential? Don't we want to make our mark on the world and to become great? Even for those immersed in materialistic pursuits, isn't it really a status symbol? Isn't it our way of showing the world that we are successful?

But what is greatness? Is true greatness only limited by a basketball shot, an exotic sports car, or a big pay check? Is there a greatness which goes beyond the world we live in? Is there a form of greatness so powerful, that it isn't even limited by our lifetime? In short, if greatness is what we all seek, why not go for the greatest form of greatness of all? Why not go for an eternal greatness?

The Jewish View on Potential

Let us turn our attention for a moment to the very beginning of the Torah in the book of Genesis. When God was creating the world, at the end of each day it is written "God looked at His creation and it was good." However, on the sixth day after the creation of man it is written "God looked at His creation and it was *very* good." Why the significant change in the wording when it came to the creation of man? Herein lies one of the fundamental beliefs of the entire Bible, and much of the reason the Bible was written to begin with. For it is *only* Man who has the ability to, indeed, become *very* good. All other creations lie only in the world of instinct and exist primarily on a simple self-serving model. It is Man, and Man alone, who has the capacity to reach greatness, to use his intellect and soul to contribute to the world and get close to His Creator. It is only Man who has the ability to transcend the mundane and reach extraordinary heights.

However, man alone cannot do it. It is very much a dual partnership. It is interesting to note that when the Torah discusses the creation of Man, it is written "Let *Us* make Man." This has always been one of the most puzzling verses in the Torah, and many Bible critics are quick to say that it shows there are multiple authors of the Torah. For why else is it written in the plural? Wasn't God the only one to write the Torah? Wasn't He the only one to create Man? The Chassidic masters answer beautifully. Yes, it was God alone who created our bodies, but Man can become a partner with God by elevating himself to greatness. God created the raw materials, but the potential is up to us. By God emphasizing this partnership at the very beginning of the Torah, God is emphasizing His belief in us that we can rise to the challenge to reach the potential He placed inside of us. But it is only with His help. By putting our trust in Him, by turning to Him for help, we become partners with God in the creation of the world and of ourselves. This idea will further be expounded in the chapter on connecting to God through creativity.

From the beginning, the Torah focuses on God believing in the potential within Man. Let us examine the first Jew who ever lived, the great Patriarch Abraham. Abraham went against the grain of the world and discovered monotheism at a young age. He looked up at the stars, and understood what no one else in the world at the time believed in; there was not a pantheon of co-existing gods who created everything and were constantly competing with each other, there was one God, who created one Reality. God wanted to test Abraham so he gave him ten trials, which would prove Abraham's love and faith in Him.

The last of these ten trials was the *Akeidah*, the Binding of Isaac. The *Akeidah* was when God asked Abraham to offer his beloved child Isaac as a sacrifice to God. Abraham obeyed and ties his son Isaac to the Alter he built on Mount Moriah. As Abraham lifted the knife to slaughter his beloved child, an angel came and stopped him at the last moment. The angel's words when he stopped him were "Abraham, Abraham!"

The commentators ask, why the need for repeated Abraham's name twice? We know the Torah does not waste words, so why in this case was his name repeated twice?

The answer the *Midrash* gives is quite startling: Each one of us is in reality two beings. There is the physical manifestation of our bodies here on this earth, and there is the spiritual representation in the World Above. Our spiritual representation above is the *ideal* Man, it is the person we are striving to become. In short, it is us at our very best, it is the person we have the potential to become. The *Midrash* explains that the reason Abraham's name was repeated is because at that moment the Abraham here on this earth *exactly* matched the Abraham of the world above. In short, Abraham had reached his full potential. It was only then that God revealed to Abraham that he was to become the father of a new nation, a nation which would become God's chosen. God knew all along Abraham had the potential inside of him; he just had to create a way for Abraham to believe in himself. The ten trials proved to Abraham that he was indeed worthy to become the father of the Jewish People, and he was ready to enter into the covenant with God.

So now for a brief word on how to view our beautiful faith. Imagine you are given a beautiful crystal gem to hold in your hand. You examine the gem in the sunlight. You see that there are so many facets to the crystal, each unique in their own way. Each facet has a different shape and contour and reflects light in a different way. Each facet shimmers and glimmers with its own beauty and color. After studying each facet, you come to appreciate and understand the full kaleidoscope of beauty which comprises this gem.

So it is with this book. The crystal gem, of course, is Judaism. Each chapter of this book will examine many of the facets to the gem that is Judaism. Whether the facet is the Sabbath, Kindness, Torah, Prayer, Redemption, each facet is revealed in a way to help us discover the beautiful gem that Judaism offers. In time, we will come to fully understand and appreciate the gem that has been placed into our hands. As the great *Ramchal* (Rabbi Moses Chaim Luzzatto) once wrote, I offer little in this book that is new, only uncovering what we deep down already know. I believe that each of these chapters will not only illuminate some of the most beautiful concepts in Judaism, but will serve as a springboard to help us reach greatness.

The Potential Within Man

And now a brief word on advice from a great sage on how we are to view ourselves. Rabbi Nachman of Breslov writes the following parable. Someone once had a dream of a great treasure chest buried underneath a certain bridge in a distant city. He travelled with great difficulty to the far away city, and after much time was able to locate the bridge he remembered from his dream. When he found the guard who watched over the bridge, he described the dream, and asked permission to begin digging under the bridge. The guard smiled smugly. He told him, it is quite ironic, because he had a dream last night, about someone from a faraway land coming to him, who has a hidden treasure chest in his own yard! The man returned home, and began digging. Sure enough, he found the treasure he had dreamed about in his own property!

The parable is short and simple, but contains some of the most profound ideas about life and the world we live in. Many of us continue searching daily for some far away fix, for something we dream will help us with life, with fulfillment, with happiness, with reaching our potential. Many people spend countless number of dollars each year on these fixes, determined to find the answers we seek.

The irony of course, is that most of what we seek is already inside of us! We were built with tremendous potential; we were built with the capacity for happiness and fulfillment. Travelling to far off distant lands, to spend exorbitant amounts of money to search for happiness and fulfillment often does little except to make us poorer and more frustrated. The guard of the bridge in the parable is just revealing what each of us already knows deep down is true.

It is the parable about each one of us. So often we don't *live* life, we merely *walk through* life, struggling with our own self-doubts and insecurities. We so often think we just were born to be simple, to struggle, to remain insignificant. Much worse, we often look at only the successes of others and say "Well, this person is obviously gifted, unlike me. They must have been born with the ability to accomplish great things. I must learn to accept my fate as a person without any real talents or skills." However, nothing could be further from the truth. Inside each and every one of us, there is a soul yearning for greatness, with potential for greatness. This treasure isn't something we have to seek; it is already inside of us! The Torah compares each man to a tree in a field, one only need to water it and care for it, and the tree can produce fruits and reach extraordinary heights.

Rabbi Binyomin Shafier tells the story of a woman named Laura Shultz from Tallahassee, Florida, who, in 1977 picked up the front of a Buick to save a young boy trapped underneath it. The most astonishing part of the story was that the woman was the boy's 63-year-old grandmother! The woman said she didn't remember picking up anything in her life heavier than 50 pounds, and yet the front of the Buick was estimated to be 2000 pounds. Dr. Charles Garfield, a well-known author, wanted to interview the woman. At first the woman refused to be interviewed, and only agreed after much coaxing from Dr. Garfield. During the interview, Dr. Garfield asked her why she had been so reluctant to get interviewed. She replied that she didn't like to think about it because it challenged her beliefs about what she could and couldn't do, about what was possible. Her words were: "If I was able to do this when I didn't think I could, what does that say about the rest of my life? Have I wasted my life?" Dr. Garfield asked her if there were things in her life she wished she could have accomplished. Mrs. Shultz responded that she always wished she could have gone to college to study geology, since she was always fascinated by the study of rocks. With some coaching from Dr. Garfield, Laura Shultz went on to earn a master's degree and teach courses at a college level.

What an inspiring story about hidden potential! If this was true for Laura Shultz, isn't it true for all of us? The sad part is that many of us have been conditioned for many years that we can only go so far in life, to reach our goals, to become great. It is not that we are limited by our conditions; it is the preconceived conditions that limit us! Rabbi Shafier gives a wonderful analogy about an elephant. The elephant is still used to this day in India as a way to carry heavy burdens, wares, etc. An elephant is a very strong animal capable of carrying enormous weights. And yet, every night its owner ties it to a tiny peg in the ground. Incredibly, the elephant stays tied to it, and does not even attempt to break free from the peg. How does such a condition come about? The answer is quite startling. When the elephant is a little baby, its owner would tie it to a small peg in the ground each night. The baby elephant would try to break free and would be unable to do it. As such, it becomes conditioned at a young age that it is never able to break free from the small peg in the ground, even as the elephant grows much bigger and stronger.

A similar concept exists with horses. At a young age, a baby horse is put by its owner in a field with a wooden fence around it. The baby horse tries to escape by leaping over the fence, but is unable to do so. The horse, similar to the elephant, becomes conditioned for life that it will never be able to jump over that fence, even as it grows bigger and stronger.

Sounds ridiculous to us, doesn't it? But is it really that far from the human condition? How many of us remained tied for our lives to a tiny peg in the ground, thinking we are unable to break free? How many of us remain prisoners of our own devices, afraid to take the leap over the fence that surrounds us? Are we really limited by our condition, or does our view of our condition limit us?

What does Judaism have to say about this? The answer can be found in the greatest leader the Jewish People ever had. We are taught at the end of the Five Books of Moses that there has never been and never will be a leader quite like Moses. Never will there be a prophet as great as Moses, who saw God "face to face" as the Torah says, which is limited by our understanding, but nonetheless speaks volumes about his spiritual heights. As a leader, he brought an entire nation out of bondage and to Mt. Sinai to receive the Torah and paved the way to bring them to the Promised Land. And yet, early into the Moses story we are taught he had a speech impediment. Moses was *aral sefatayim*, commonly translated "of uncircumcised of the lips," as he was probably painful to listen to. At first he didn't believe in himself, and God chastised him for that. If God can believe in him, shouldn't he believe in himself? And eventually he did, and he rose to the level that he did. He was only able to reach his potential when he realized how much God believed in Him. It is only when we come to understand how great we can become, that we begin to accomplish what seems to be the impossible.

The Purpose of this Book

And now, as you Dear Reader are still trying to figure out what to make of this book, let me tell you what this book is *not*. This book is *not* a so-called self-help book. It is not a book claiming to contain 'All of the Answers to Life's Questions in 300 Pages or Less,' as other books claim. Those kinds of books contain countless numbers of claims, most of which are nothing more than sleazy sales pitches, and each more ludicrous than the last; "10 Days till a Brand New You!," "The Secrets to Success and Personal Power" "Free Yourself from Anxiety the Easy Way," "5 Rules for Love and Happiness," and the list goes on. One can become dizzy just from glancing from one title to the next. Pretty amazing to think all of life's problems will be solved for a mere $15.99 plus tax! This book, I assure you, makes no such claims.

Now, let me start to tell you what this book *is*. Above all, this book is meant to inspire. It will help to illuminate some of the most beautiful and deepest concepts in Judaism, but will not solve all of life's problems and questions. It is merely meant to bring solace and comfort, and help people develop a stronger connection to their Creator. Yes, it is true that I hope everyone who reads this book will become a better person, and will find much comfort in its pages.

Beyond that, its purpose lies solely with the reader. This book is a seed and soil, but the sunlight and water must be provided by you, and the flower can take a lifetime to grow. The concepts are meant to serve as a spring board to reach greatness, but that is still takes a lifetime of hard work. Good things, real important things in life, career, love, marriage, and children take a lifetime of hard work, nothing is ever spoon-fed to us. Certainly the same is true of spiritual growth as well.

I heard an amazing anecdote from Rabbi Binny Friedman. There was a great rabbi known as the Alter (Elder) of Slobodka. The Alter lived during very difficult times in Europe, and yet he still managed despite impossible odds, to build *yeshivot,* schools of religious study. When asked how he was able to accomplish this, he gave a startling and insightful answer. He said "I didn't think about whether or not I can do it, I thought *about whether or not it needs to be done.*" This is brilliance, and it contains the secret to accomplishing great things. When the focus solely becomes on me, then all of my self-doubts start to creep in and the task can seem very daunting indeed. But when the focus is solely on the mission, on the end result, then anything is possible! When one envisions the end result, and knows that this *needs* to be done, it is not a matter of *if*, it is a matter of *when.* You have begun to climb the mountain without ever looking back. I want to expand upon this idea even more. When a person remains connected only to oneself, then the more difficult and arduous the task will seem. But when one uses his self to connect wholly to Judaism, then he is connecting to something much greater than himself. When one does this, the potential is practically limitless. He is tapping into resources from a tradition that is boundless in spiritual energy. I hoped, when writing this book, to tap into this beautiful tradition that is our faith, and invite you to tap into it together with me.

Reaching Beyond Ourselves

There is an amazing story in one of my favorite books *Chassidic Tales of the Holocaust* by Yaffa Eliach. The story is told about Rabbi Yisroel Spira, also known as the Bloushiver Rebbe. The story is about a cruel game the Nazis were playing on the inmates in one of the camps. The inmates were forced to make a nearly impossible leap across a massive pit. For those who made it to the other side, their lives were spared. For those who did not, the pit became their grave.

Rabbi Spira stood at edge of the pit. Next to him, was a secular Jew he had befriended in the camp. Rabbi Spira closed his eyes and took the leap. Impossibly, he made it to the other side. Even more incredibly, the secular Jew who was with him made it to the other side as well. The secular Jew asked Rabbi Spira how he was able to make the jump. Rabbi Spira responded "I was hanging onto the coat tails of our great ancestors, Abraham, Isaac, and Jacob. I was hanging onto my grandparents and great-grandparents. But how, my friend, did you make the jump?" The secular Jew responded "I was hanging onto your coat tail."

This poignant story contains what is one of life's greatest lessons when it comes to reaching our potential. As long as we think it is *just us* who is making the leap, we can never do it, indeed often the leap is too difficult. But when we latch onto something much greater than ourselves, when we latch onto a faith that is *eternal,* we can do almost anything! The sky is the limit, if not higher. Asking God for help in everything we do is the first step toward achieving greatness.

But to achieve greatness, one must always remember asking God for help certainly isn't enough on its own. Life is a balancing act, a balancing act between *bitachon* (faith) and *hishtadlut* (human effort). Only when we do our part can God come down and do the rest.

We see this idea in the story of Noah. Noah, as we know, was commanded to build an ark to protect him and his family, along with many of the animals from the oncoming Flood. The question is, how was so many species of animals able to fit in such a small ark? The answer, the *Midrash* says, was that it was indeed a miracle. The animals under normal circumstances would not have been able to all fit, but God made a miracle that in fact, all of the animals fit. Rabbeinu Bachya asks; if this were the case, then why bother having Noah create the ark at all? Why did he need to work so hard for so many years to build the ark in the first place, and why didn't God just create the ark on His own? If He was already going to do one miracle, why not just do one more? The answer, Rabbeinu Bachya says, is that we must always do our share. We cannot rely on God's miracles. We do our part as best as we can, and only then, does God come down so to speak, and help us do the rest. So when we build our own little arks inside of ourselves, to escape the floods of this world, and build a new world for ourselves rich with our own potential, we work our hardest to do our part. And then have faith and pray that God will come down and help us do the rest.

This is why I wrote this book. Above all else, this book is to help us both to reach our greatness. It certainly isn't just a journey for you; it is a journey for me as well. I am just inviting you to come along with me on the ride. What many people, including myself, are going to learn in the pages of this book is that has been a course already given to us which shows us just how great a person can become. The path has been here long before we were ever born. In fact, the path was created even before the world as we know it, came into existence. The journey is certainly a long and arduous one, but the promises of riches are beyond what we can even begin to perceive. The goal of this book is to help uncover the path, remove the brush and shrubs which have clouded it for so many for so many years. This path is a path handed down to us throughout the millennia, often in secrecy, and often with the threat or pain of death. It also has been handed down at times in glorious and triumphant moments as well. This path has a destination, and the destination is *eternal greatness.* This path is called Judaism. What this book, hopefully will show, is not only how beautiful the destination is, but the journey as well.

This may not always be so apparent; one must often dig deeply to uncover the hidden treasures. This may sometimes take a very long time for the discoveries to come, but they are there, waiting to be found. In my journey, it took many years. Although I was born into a traditionally observant home, and attended some of the finest *yeshivot* and day schools, it still took a while to discover the full richness and depth that Judaism has to offer. Although I had poured over pages of the Talmud and Bible ever since I was a little boy, Judaism, moreover my relationship to God, eluded me. Many of my discoveries took place my year in Israel. Only in Israel was I able to see the full vastness and colorful palette which comprise our People. Here I discovered and experienced Jews from all walks of life; from the Ultra-Orthodox, to the Chassidim of Chabad and Breslov, to the secular Jews, to the religious Zionists and their passionate love for the Land of Israel, to the *ba'alei teshuvah* (newly observant), to the holy soldiers who protect our land from dangerous enemies. Here in the Land of our Forefathers, where the Prophets of yesteryear walked, my great epiphany occurred. In *yeshiva*, I had discovered my intellect; in the Land of Israel I had discovered my soul.

Notice, as I mentioned earlier, I never said Judaism

is easy. At times it certainly requires a lot of diligence, whether it is fasting on Yom Kippur or the other fast days, or cleaning out one's home from *chametz* (unleavened bread crumbs) before the holiday of Passover. (Getting up early for the morning prayers has always been my struggle.) But yet there is something very fulfilling and gratifying in it all.

A few short words about the numerous quotes found throughout the book. Many of the ideas contained in this book are not my own; I am a mere scribe for the great leaders and teachers that brought these insights down into this world. I try to organize their thoughts into one collected whole. I hope and pray that their words inspire you as much as they have inspired me.

Recognizing Our Teachers

In addition, I try to quote the name of the person who told me each of the stories contained in this book. Rabbi Nachman used to say that many people tell stories to put someone to sleep, but a real story is supposed to wake someone up. I try to tell stories in this book that not only are beautiful in content, but can inspire and convey powerful lessons to help make us (myself included) into better people.

One final word about the teachers quoted in this book. In *Pirkei Avot* (Ethics of Our Fathers) it is written, "Make for yourself a teacher and acquire for yourself a friend." Indeed we are no one without teachers and friends. Thankfully I have been privileged to have many teachers, both those who I have met and those who I have only met through their prolific writings. Many of my teachers are still alive and well today, but others left this world, but are still alive through their great teachings. The Talmud quotes a verse that says "The lips of the righteous stir in the grave." This means, the Talmud explains, that whenever a teaching is said from a righteous person who has passed away, that righteous person stirs in the next world for it is through his teachings that his legacy lives on, and it is *as if* he is alive that day and his lips stir from saying the teaching. Thus it is a privilege and honor for me to be able to say over teachings and keep these people alive inside of all of us.

Furthermore, the Talmud writes that whoever says over a teaching in someone else's name brings redemption to the world. This, the Talmud writes, is seen from the Book of Esther when Esther told King Ahasureus *in the name of Mordechai* about the plot to assassinate the king. This eventually led to the great redemption of the Jewish People when they were saved from annihilation in the story of Purim. So I always try to say each teaching and story with the name of the source that I heard or read it from.

So I am grateful for my many teachers, both those who I have been privileged to meet and study under, and those who have only taught me after they had passed from this world. Several individuals stand above others for making the greatest impact on me, and I feel imperative to acknowledge, that for the little that I do know about this world and our faith, I owe to them.

Now, I have another special soul to thank, my Sweet Kelly. Where would I be today without my Kelly, standing by my side and encouraging me every step of the way? A true measure of someone's greatness is when the more you uncover, the more treasures you find. I have only just begun to get to know my wife Kelly and the more I have uncovered, the more depth and beauty I see. Thank you for coming into my life. You are my best friend.

I am grateful to Rabbi Moshe Weinberger who led me to see the beauty of Chassidut. A great Chassidic master once said, "There are some souls which are vessels to receive the Light, and there are some great souls who are the Light itself." Such can be said about Rabbi Moshe Weinberger, whose rays continue to spread to the four corners of the earth. He has opened gates for me that I didn't even know existed. My Judaism has never been the same. So many of the teachings contained in this book I have heard from him.

In the world of music, Rabbi Shlomo Carlebach stands alone as the one who has taught me the power of the melody. A person's greatness is often measured by how long it takes for people to understand and appreciate their genius. He inspired me to write and record my own melodies. Our generation is just beginning to glimpse the depth of his musical brilliance.

Of the Chassidic masters, Rabbi Menachem Mendel Schneerson, of blessed memory, has spread Judaism to the world in ways that no one would have ever dreamed possible. Although, I am not strictly Chabad, I have ever-greatening appreciation for his many contributions and teachings. The Talmud says that when I righteous person leaves the world, it is like a person losing a pearl. The pearl only remains lost to the owner, but the pearl still exists. The Rebbe's soul is still very much alive, and we continue to feel his presence when we study his teachings.

In the world of art, two names stand out in my mind: Channan Baer, how can I forget where it all began? Chana, thanks for your endless guidance with watercolors and calligraphy. I am eternally grateful for you for seeing that spark inside of me and bringing it to fruition and for opening my eyes up to the colors of the palette.

But the biggest thanks I have saved for last. Ever since I was a little boy, my parents have always been there for me. I remember well my father coming home after a long hard day at work and sitting down with me in front of the *alef-bet*. He taught me *Chumash*, the great stories of the origins of our people. And while my father taught me the *knowledge* of Judaism, my mother taught me the *sweetness* of Judaism, as she sang to me beautiful melodies to help put me to sleep every night. I cannot thank them enough. The little I have accomplished in life, I owe completely to them. Thank you for lifting me up in a thousand ways, and for always believing in me.

But finally the greatest thank you of all goes to God, who has given me the beautiful gift of being able to create paintings, music, speaking, and writing that can inspire others. While drawing, singing, speaking, and writing I can feel Your Hand guiding my hand and voice and I can feel Your Everlasting Love as You whisper in my ear words of encouragement.

Before I complete this introduction, I wanted to share a word to all of you Dear Readers who have picked up this book. The great mystic and Kabbalist of Safed, Rabbi Isaac Luria, best known as the Arizal, once called over his prized pupil Rabbi Chaim Vital, and said to him a remarkable statement. He said, "You are a very holy person, for you have chosen, in a world full of physical and material lures, to study by my side and learn the ancient Jewish wisdom and texts from me." I begin with this vignette because of how much more true this is today! We live in a world with far greater temptations than sixteenth-century Safed, and yet, you Dear Reader, have chosen to pick up this book on Jewish spirituality and wisdom. This is something you deserve to be commended for.

Since so much of what I will quote from is from my beloved teacher Rabbi Moshe Weinberger, it is only apropos that I begin with a story he once said. Years ago in England, there used to be a poetry contest for who could recite a poem in the most eloquent fashion. One year, the poem that was chosen was Psalm 23, the famous Psalm "The Lord is my Shepherd, I shall not want." One young man, trained in Shakespearean prose, recited the Psalm beautifully, and was declared the winner of the contest.

As they were about to hand him the award, an old Jewish man in the audience spoke in broken English, "Can I try to recite the Psalm?" The man had a heavy European accent, and he looked unkempt. After much murmuring, the judges decided to allow the man to recite the Psalm. The man began the Psalm in his heavily accented broken English. At first, the audience was a little disgusted, but soon they began to feel the incredible raw emotion that flowed from the man's voice. It soon became clear that this man wasn't reciting the Psalm, he was living it. When he finished the Psalm, there was silence in the audience. Some had begun to cry. In a moment, it was clear that he was the true winner of the contest. The man who was given the award walked to the old man who read the Psalm and tried to offer the award, but the old man refused. 'Tell me, how did you learn to recite that Psalm the way you did?" The old man was quiet for a moment before he responded. "It is very simple. I know the Shepherd."

This is another reason why I wrote this book. The book is to help everyone (including myself) get to know the Shepherd. The world as we know it is transient. Our days are fleeting. It is written in the liturgy of the High Holy Days, "Man's origin is from dust, and his destiny is back to dust, at risk of his life he earns his bread; he is likened to a broken shard, withering grass, a fading flower, a passing shade...." It is up to us to develop a relationship with our Maker in the little bit of time that we have. This is why we are here in this world.

This book is my passion; it is my artwork, my music, my heart, and soul poured out into the written word. It is over seven years in the making; whenever I had a free moment, be it on the subway, during my lunch break, or at home or while sipping coffee at Starbucks I would pour my thoughts and emotions onto paper. Often I would find that when I would express myself on paper it had an even stronger effect than when I expressed myself on canvas or with my guitar. Some of the greatest moments of my life were spent filling up these pages. I felt closer to God more than ever before in my entire life, except the day of my wedding. Rabbi Abraham Isaac Kook says that to make the world a better place one cannot chase away darkness, one must light a candle. I wrote this book to try to bring meaning, purpose, fulfillment, and ultimately happiness to those who read it. May this book serve as an inspiration for all of those who are seeking to get a taste of how beautiful Judaism can be.

Much of this book contains my own journey to discovering the beauties of Judaism, and therefore it is my own personal story. But in a sense we are all authors. We are authors of our own story. The chapters of our lives are continuously being written by the decisions we make. We each hold our own pen, and what the contents of our own pages will be remains entirely up to us. Our choices are what our stories become. We choose our own destiny. The positive deeds we do makes our story happy and life affirming; when we give in to our failings and shortcomings our story becomes more tragic.

One word about the name of this book, and the pastel drawing I did for the cover. The drawing is based on a well-known inspirational photograph, and it right away struck me as being perfect for the book cover. I felt it is a father and son, the older generation and the younger generation walking on a path together, in the quiet of the forest during daybreak, with the rays of sun poking through the trees. It really is true that sometimes a picture says a thousand words. I named this book *The Hidden Path* for I feel that is what Judaism is. In fact, the word *halachah,* which we commonly translate as "Jewish law," in reality, means "the way," as it comes from the word *holech,* "to go." Thus Judaism is more than just a mere religion; it is a way of life. "Its ways are ways of pleasantness and all its paths are peace," as the verse writes. Judaism doesn't leave us when we leave the synagogue and study hall; it follows us every moment of our day and lives, from the moment we get up in the morning till the moment we go to sleep. Thus this explains the painting I did for the cover. I feel it also captures the idea of the older generation leading and teaching the younger generation the proper Path of Life. So much in Judaism as we know focuses on educating our children on what the Torah says, "You shall teach your children and speak these words," as we say every day in the *Shema*. Everything in Judaism focuses on *Mesorah,* on teaching the tradition to the next generation. This goes back even to Moses on Mount Sinai, as it is written in the beginning of *Pirkei Avot* (Ethics of our Fathers) where it says that Moses taught the Torah to Joshua, and Joshua to the Elders, and so on. The *Mesorah,* tradition, is the bedrock of our faith.

Rabbi Eliezer Azikiri wrote in his song "Beloved of Your Soul":

Please be revealed and spread upon me, my Beloved, the shelter of Your peace. Illuminate the world with Your glory that we may rejoice and be glad with You. Hasten, show us love, for the time has come, and show us grace as in the days of old.

Strength and love to all. Meet you at the end of the Path.

Best wishes,
Yisroel Juskowitz
Rockville, MD 2013

Chapter 1
Seeing God Everywhere (Even in the Most Unlikely of Places)

Earth is crammed with Heaven,
And every common bush is afire with God;
But only he who sees takes off his shoes.

~ Elizabeth Barrett Browning

WHEN WE ARE YOUNG CHILDREN, we speak to God, and feel He is a friend to which we can turn to. We are able to look out at the beauty in the world, and understand that it all came from God. I remember as a young child, standing next to my windowsill every night and talking to God out the window into the open night air. There is nothing more innocent and pure than a young child, and the wonder with which they look at the world. Children are born totally dependent in everything they do.

But as we grow older, and grow our own independence, we begin to lose any sense of dependency, and in turn, any sense of innocence. We often become arrogant with our accomplishments, and sometimes cynical toward anything spiritual or Godlike. Our practical side takes over; we are overcome with the bleak intoxications of daily living. We think only of how we are going to pay the bills, pick up the groceries, and help our kids with their homework. Awareness of God's Presence starts to slip away. Where is God today, in our everyday lives? Does He live in us, as the Torah teaches? What can we do in our lives to feel His Presence more?

The way to begin to see God in everything begins with a paradigm shift in how we look at the world. Many people adhere to the phrase "Seeing is Believing." But in reality, the opposite order is true. If you Believe, then you will See. If you believe firmly in God, you begin to see God in everything around us, and in everything we do. Not only do we begin to see God in His creations, but we begin to see Him in our actions as well.

Seeing God Through Our Actions

Rabbi Berel Wein told over the following tragic but uplifting story. For one moment, let us be transported to the harrowing days of the Second World War, where God seemed to turn a deaf ear to the cries of His people. In the confines of the Warsaw Ghetto, a woman and her son were hounded by the SS for weeks, constantly on the run, barely alive. Finally an SS officer found them, managing to chase them into a dusty dirty attic in one of the dilapidated homes in the Ghetto. Narrowed into a corner, the young child in a fit of terror and rage suddenly turned on the Nazi officer and seized him by the throat. The officer, gasping for air, went limp, completely at the child's mercy. At this point, the mother leapt out from where she was, and yelled to the child, "No! Don't kill him! We are not killers!"

What became of this young boy and her mother is unknown. But this short story teaches us some of the greatest lessons known to man. One cannot even imagine the holiness that emanated from that room at that moment. According to Jewish Law the child would have been in complete right to kill the officer; the Talmud dictates that when someone is attempting to kill you, you can kill that person first in self defense, but still it was difficult for them to do it. We are not killers. It is hard for us. Perhaps what occurred in that room was even greater than all of the majesty of divine revelation at Mount Sinai. At Mount Sinai the goal of "Thou shalt not kill" was proclaimed, there in that dusty dirty attic in the Ghetto that goal was fulfilled in its ultimate form.

Here we see that even in the most forlorn places in the world, God's Presence is revealed. God's Presence is revealed through the actions of His People. We get just a glimpse of the incredible greatness that is inherent within Man, a glimmer of the Divine Image within, and the spiritual levels that man can attain.

So this is where our journey begins; finding God everywhere even in the most unlikely of places. Every one of us at some point in our lives, have felt God's comforting hand on our shoulder, sometimes in times of joy and sometimes in times of sadness. The Kotzker Rebbe was once asked by a Chassid, "Where can God be found?" The Kotzker Rebbe answered that God can be found wherever one lets him in. It is written in the verse in Isaiah "You are My witnesses, I am God." What does this cryptic verse mean? As long as we remain God's witnesses, he remains our God. But when we no longer allow ourselves to witness, He is not God. This doesn't mean that He doesn't exist; it means that in our own narrow perspective of the world, He doesn't exist.

This sheds light on a very enigmatic statement in the Talmud. The Talmud writes, "All is in the hands of Heaven except yireh (fear) of Heaven." The Hebrew word yireh is commonly translated "fear," or "awe," but it can also mean "see." Thus, this means all is in the hands of Heaven, except "seeing" Heaven. Everything in our life is already predetermined. But seeing God? Being aware of his presence? That is up to us. We can choose to see God in our everyday lives, or we can choose not to. What we decide makes all the difference in the world in determining what type of lifestyle we will lead.

Seeing God in Nature

We see God through looking at His beautiful world. King David wrote in the book of Psalms, "There is no Rock (*Tzur*) like our God." The Talmud says don't read it *tzur*, but rather *tziar*, "artist." So the verse reads "There is no Artist like our God." Indeed, who hasn't marveled at the majestic mountains, the colors of the rainbow after an afternoon shower, a glorious sunset, the break of dawn, the thousands of species of wildlife and fish that God has sculpted into existence? King David wrote in Psalms, "He sends the springs into the streams, they flow between the mountains. They water every beast of the field, they quench the wild creatures' thirst. Near them dwell the heaven's birds, from among the branches they give forth song. He waters the mountains from his upper chambers, from the fruit of your work the earth is sated." These verses give us a small taste of the beauty of God's creations.

The key is to recognize that all of nature is a testimony to God's Greatness. I heard from Rabbi Tzvi Hirsch Weinreb on the last day of Passover, which is the day according to Jewish tradition that the Red Sea was split, a parable from the Klausenberger Rebbe. A great sculptor wanted to make a masterpiece for which he would always be remembered. He decided to sculpt a horse. He spent time carefully studying the anatomy of a horse, and then put a countless number of hours into sculpting it, careful to create every curve to absolute perfection. When the horse was completed, it looked absolutely magnificent. He decided to leave the horse in the middle of the road on the way to the marketplace for everyone to see. Expecting a great reaction from all who passed it, the sculptor was shocked when everyone just walked right by it and ignored it! It looked so realistic that everyone thought it was just a regular horse. Frustrated, the sculptor decided to cut the horse in half. Now when everyone walked by it, they stared at it in awe and said "Wow! Now *that* is a horse!" So it is with the miracle of the splitting the sea. It took a miracle of that magnitude to appreciate God's Greatness, when really we are witness to His Power every time when we walk by the sea and gaze out at its immense beauty. The sea, with all of its thousands of species of fish, its colorful corals and reefs, and magnificent waves, is a miracle in and of itself.

There is an enigmatic passage in *Pirkei Avot* (Ethics of Our Fathers). The passage reads, "If one was traveling on the road while studying Torah and interrupted his studies to exclaim, 'What a beautiful tree!' Scripture views it as if he bears guilt for his soul." How are we to understand this passage? Isn't it virtuous to appreciate God's world? What sin did this person commit? Rabbi Abraham Isaac Kook explains the passage beautifully. The key word is that is says he *interrupted* his studies. Instead of viewing the world as a continuation of God's Holiness, he viewed Nature as separate from God's Holiness. However, the reality is that studying Torah is one channel to get close to God, and admiring God's world is another. This means the real way to view Torah and the physical world is not as a *separation,* but as a *continuation* of experiencing the Divine. This was the mistake that this person made in the passage from *Pirkei Avot*.

One teaching which demonstrates the idea of seeing God everywhere is the verse, "The world is full of Your Acquiring." What does this verse mean? Surely we know that God owns everything in the world! Rabbi Tzadok HaKohen interpreted the verse homiletically. The verse means that *the whole earth is full of ways to acquire God.* One must only open his eyes to see it. The verse writes, "Holy, holy, holy is the Lord of Hosts, for the whole earth is filled with His Glory." Thus we see the deep connection between holiness and earth. We see God's Holiness from appreciating the world.

The Greatness of God lies in His ability to create multitudes of creations, each unique and colorful. The Talmud writes, "Great is the Holy One Blessed is He, for when man mints a coin, all subsequent coins look exactly like the original, but when God created Adam, all of his descendants are different from one another."

Seeing Our Dependency on Him

So we develop our closeness to God by admiring the beauty of His creations, by studying His word, and by realizing that without God, we are nothing. We need him so desperately for everything. One of the most incredible insights I ever heard came from a mentor of mine, Rabbi Yitzchok Dinowitzer. In the prayer *Nishmat Kol Chai* ("The Soul of Every Living Being), it says, "Were our mouth as full of song as the sea, and our tongue as full of joyous song as its multitude of waves, and our lips as full of praise as the breath of the heavens, and our eyes as brilliant as the sun and the moon, and our hands as outspread as eagles of the sky and our feet as swift as hinds, we still *could not* thank You sufficiently *Hashem* our God, and God of our forefathers, and to bless Your Name...." However, just a few sentences later it says, "Therefore, the organs that You set within us, and the spirit and soul that that You breathed into our nostrils, and the tongue that You placed in our mouth, all of them *shall thank and bless*, praise and glorify, exalt and revere, sanctify and declare the sovereignty of Your Name, our King." How are we to reconcile this discrepancy? On the one hand we say that we do not have the ability to thank and bless God, and yet just a few sentences later we do just that! Rabbi Dinowitzer says that the answer lies within the sentences themselves. We are not *able* to adequately thank God because *everything* we have is His. The most we can do is use the organs that He gave us to praise Him. It is the equivalent of a son who loves his father so dearly but he can't give him a gift since everything he owns really belongs to his father, so the most he could do is ask his father for his credit card and use that to buy his father a gift! We see this in the very same words, "Therefore, the organs that *You set within us*, and the spirit and soul that that *You breathed into our nostrils*, and the tongue that *You placed in our mouth*, all of them shall thank and bless... sovereignty of Your Name, our King." Spiritual awareness begins with realizing that without God we cannot *live,* he is the life force that sustains all of us. This is as the Zohar writes, "It is You Who nourishes all and sustains all; You control everything. It is You Who control Kings, and kingship is Yours."

Bringing Meaning to the Physical World

Suddenly, with the realization that everything we have is His, life takes on a whole new meaning. Everything in the physical world has potential for spirituality; everything can either be elevated for a higher purpose, or just remain part of the physical realm. We see this concept in a contradiction between a Jewish teaching and Jewish Law. In *Pirkei Avot* (Ethics of our Fathers) it writes, "Eat bread with salt, drink water in small measure, sleep on the ground, live a life of deprivation—but toil in the Torah!" However, we know that Judaism is replete with examples of indulging in physical pleasures! On the Sabbath according to Jewish Law one is supposed to eat in with the choicest meat, finest wine, and finest table-settings. Indeed, many of the greatest of the Talmudic sages used to save as much money as they could during the week in order to have the most extravagant Sabbath meal. Nearly all of the Jewish holidays are replete with festive meals. How are we to reconcile these discrepancies?

Once again, within the question, lies the answer. Judaism believes that the physical pleasures of the world can be meaningless if that is the end goal itself. In such a case, there is nothing more detrimental to one's soul than the materialistic world that we live in. However, the physical world can *take on infinite meaning* if elevated for a higher purpose. If the goal of the physical world is to bring one closer to God by fulfilling His will in the most beautiful way possible, then there is no higher state of existence than the physical world that we live in. Suddenly, everything takes on new meaning! Every object, every desire is now something that should necessarily be avoided, but something that can bond us to our Creator.

This is the eternal message of Judaism; to elevate that which is mundane, to not allow that which is physical to remain just purely physical. We see this also in regards to indulging in sexual pleasures. On the one hand the Torah condemns sexually immoral behavior, but yet numerous times the Torah emphasizes the marriage imperative, and the importance and sanctity of marriage. There is an obligation according to Jewish Law to try to satisfy their partner's sexual needs to the best of their ability. There is even a *mitzvah* to engage in intimate relations with one's spouse on the Sabbath night. In fact, the very first commandment of the Torah is to be fruitful and multiply, indicating the importance of procreation and therefore needing a sexual relationship. The sexual organs are one of the faculties which we are created with, which can either be used for total selfishness and debauchery or it can elevate us to express love and to bring down children into this world.

It is interesting to note that the Torah doesn't command us to be spiritual; it commands us to be *holy.* Holiness is not total withdrawal from the physical; it is a fusing together of the spiritual and physical. It is this very real process of channeling the physical world and the pleasures of this world into a vehicle for us to lead a Godly life.

This is why in when it comes to a mitzvah there is almost no limit to how beautiful it should be. When purchasing an *etrog,* the citrus fruit of the holiday of Sukkot, the Torah even specifies that one should buy one that is exquisitely beautiful. By the festival of Hanukkah, people go to great lengths to purchase a magnificent *menorah,* on Passover to have beautiful goblets for wine, and the list goes on. Of course, one should never go beyond one's personal means; the Torah would never expect that much, and doing so may even go against some of the precepts of the Torah.

The Torah tells us that with every *physical act* which is a mitzvah we are really connecting to a higher realm. That is why the Baal Shem Tov says that the blessing we say on each mitzvah that we contains the words, "Who has sanctified us with His *commandments.*" The Baal Shem Tov explains that the reason this is written in the plural even though one is only doing *one* mitzvah at that time is because each mitzvah that we do is really connecting to the same mitzvah in the higher world, which cannot be expressed in physical terms.

Seeing Spirituality in the Physical World

Even within the physical realm, we find hints to the spiritual world. We find the greatest hint in the drinking of wine. Rabbi Akiva Tatz writes that wine has different properties than virtually any other object in the physical world. Nearly everything within the physical world erodes or wanes with time. However, wine, which as we will see, has close links with the spiritual world, only gets better with time! This is a close link to the intellect, which houses the capacity to study the Torah, since it also generally gets better, with time. As a person ages, he usually becomes wiser and more knowledgeable.

Rabbi Tatz continues that there is an even greater correlation that wine has with the spiritual world. The Talmud relates the following remarkable story. The daughter of one of the Roman Caesars once went to one of the great Talmudic sages who was particularly unattractive and asked him, "How can it be that the Torah, which a wisdom which is so holy, be contained in an object that is so ugly?" The sage responded, "What does your father store his wine in?" She answered "Earthenware vessels." The sage then asked, "Why doesn't your father store it in something more beautiful, such as gold or silver? Wine, which is an exquisite delicacy, should not be contained in such a simple ugly vessel!" She agreed, and asked her father to transfer the wine into gold vessels. Two weeks later the wine was spoiled. The Caesar demanded to speak to the sage. "Why did you advise my daughter to pour my wine into gold vessels? The wine is spoiled now." The sage replied that when the vessel is of primary importance, the contents get ruined. So it is with Torah, the Divine Wisdom. The more important the *body* becomes, the more sunk one is into glamour and beauty, the less of a vessel he is to accept the Divine Wisdom.

We find another paradox within Judaism about wine. According to Jewish Law, a person is supposed to be careful to stay healthy as much as possible, and therefore stay away from substances which can be harmful. However, there are numerous Jewish customs and laws that center on the consumption of wine. We bring in the Sabbath with a cup of wine and we leave the Sabbath with a cup of wine. On Passover we drink four cups of wine signifying the four stages of Redemption. There is even a holiday of Purim where it is a religious obligation to drink wine, perhaps even to the point of intoxication! Yet the commentators say that Purim has the ability to bring one to a higher level of holiness than Yom Kippurim, the Jewish Day of Atonement. They explain this because the word *Kippurim* means "like Purim," meaning that Yom Kippurim can only be *similar* to Purim, but not the same elevated state that we reach on Purim. How are we to understand this? With the concept that we have been saying, wine can either be rooted purely in the physical world, which would lead man to total destruction, or it can be used for a mitzvah, for something commanded by God, it can elevate the person to otherwise unattainable heights. The Talmud says that the Hebrew word *yayin*, "wine," has the numerical value of seventy, which has the same numerical value as the word *sod*, "secret." The Talmud explains that this is because when wine enters the person, the secrets come out. This means that wine has the ability to bring out parts of the person that would never otherwise be revealed. This is why Purim has such incredible potential, perhaps even greater than Yom Kippur. Furthermore, Purim can be greater because Man is showing that he can serve God even with the physical pleasures of the world, unlike Yom Kippur, when the physical pleasures of the world are removed.

We find another example of the concept of the spiritual world being concealed within the physical realm in the property of fire. On the one hand, fire has the incredible destructive power to consume, inflict pain, and injury. On the other hand, fire has the power to create energy, light and warmth. How are we to understand this? Once again, the concept is the same. If utilized properly, fire has incredible positive potential, if not utilized properly then only the destructive properties remain. It is therefore no coincidence that the Torah is often compared to fire. The Torah writes, "Behold, my words are like fire, so says the Lord." Indeed, the book of Exodus relates that the Torah was given on Mount Sinai through fire. It is also no coincidence that much of Jewish ritual utilizes fire as a medium to connect us to God. We bring in the Sabbath with candles and we leave the Sabbath with fire. We even have the holiday of Hanukkah which centers on lighting candles.

Perhaps the greatest connection that we find in Judaism to the deeper meaning of fire is when God spoke to Moses. The Torah tells us that the burning bush that God spoke to Moses from was burning but was not consumed by the fire. Thus the fire was just providing warmth and light, but not destroying. This illustrates our concept in the most profound way. Judaism teaches that this is the ultimate purpose of fire. Fire, like virtually anything in the physical world, can be used to build, to heal and to deepen or connection with God, if utilized properly.

Perhaps now we can understand a cryptic passage in *Pirkei Avot*. The passage reads, "Warm yourself by the fire of the sages, but beware of their glowing coal lest you be burnt." With this understanding of the concept of fire, this passage is illuminated. The passage means warm yourself by their fire, meaning allow yourself to utilize the fire of Torah in the way that *it was intended,* meaning to heal, to provide warmth and light. But beware of their glowing coals lest you be burnt, meaning *don't utilize fire in the way that it was not intended*—don't get too close, don't take advantage of the sages without treating them with the proper respect and awe that they deserve, for then their fire will burn and destroy you. This is the parallel between the physical and spiritual worlds.

This is why Judaism is built on sanctifying the physical world for a higher purpose. The Talmud sites a contradiction between two verses. One the one hand, the verse says, "To God, the earth and all its glory," which implies that the entire earth belongs to God. However, there is another verse which says, "As for the heavens, heaven belongs to God, but the earth was given to man." This verse clearly states that the earth was given to man! The Talmud gives a brilliant explanation to answer the contradiction. The first verse is talking about a food *before* man made a blessing on it, but the second verse is talking about *after* man made a blessing on it. Once man makes the blessing, the food, so to speak, was *taken out* of God domain and *given* to man. Thus man has acquired the food from God. The entire earth can be thought of as God's "supermarket" and we must "purchase" a food in order to partake of it. With the concepts we have spoken about, we can now say that by making the blessing, we have elevated the food into something spiritual and it is now ours to partake of.

The great mystic Rabbi Tzadok HaKohen of Lublin writes a great deal about the potential holiness of the act of eating. He writes that it is no coincidence that in dealing with the laws of the Temple service it begins with the laws of sacrifices and ends with the laws of the Showbread, which is the part of the service most connected with food. This is because the two are comparable; when one eats properly it is as if he has offered a sacrifice to God. This is the meaning behind the Talmudic statement that one's dinner table is similar to the Altar in the Holy Temple. He continues to explain that this is why there are so many laws in Judaism comparing the table to the Altar; for instance one may not sit on the table that one eats from for it is similar to the Altar which we are to treat with the utmost respect. In addition, this is the reason for the ancient Jewish tradition to wash one's hands in a ritual fashion before eating bread, since the same process was done by the priests in the Holy Temple before preparing a sacrifice.

Rabbi Tzadok continues by quoting a story in the Talmud of one of the great sages who said that when he died worms would never devour his body because he always ate with proper intention; that is as a way to get closer to God. He declared that when he died, his intestines would cry out to the Glory of God, for he never partook of food just for the sake of indulging as an end in and of itself. This is the reason why we the last food that we are to eat on the Passover *Seder* night is the *afikoman.* God is whispering into our ears to remember to allow the spiritual food of matzah to linger in our mouths. This should be the last taste we are left with on Passover night.

Rabbi Berel Wein uses this idea and explains that this is why just at the moment of Exodus, God commanded us to eat matzah. This is because at that pivotal moment in Jewish history, when we were being forged into a nation, God wanted to instill within us that food is meant to be spiritual substance, and it can be a mitzvah, as matzah is.

Our lifelong mission is to find meaning in the physical world which we live in. Rabbi David Aaron once said that Judaism is not a religion which lingers exclusively in the past or is only for the future. True, we commemorate great events and we anticipate the future coming of the Messiah. But, in reality, Judaism is about infusing the *moment* with infinite meaning. A student of Rabbi Moshe Cabriner was once asked what his teacher's primary focus in life was.

The inquisitor expected to hear prayer, repentance, Torah study, or acts kindness. Instead, the student surprised the inquisitor with a very astute answer. He said that his teacher's primary focus was what he was doing right at that moment. The lesson is a powerful one. Every moment we have an opportunity, to do good, to show compassion, to study God's Word, to pray, to bring God closer down into this world. As *Pirkei Avot* says, "If not now, when?"

Seeking Inspiration

Rabbi Shlomo Carlebach once said that while he was composing his famous song "Open up the Gates" that it occurred to him that everyone at some point in their lives tried to knock on that door, hoping to find the closeness they needed. Sadly enough, many people walk away and don't continue to knock. The truth is that we have no choice because life without Him is empty. We must be prepared to knock for a lifetime.

Truthfully, it is hard to keep knocking. King David wrote in Psalms, "We tell of God's kindness during the day, but at night time our faith endures." This means that there are times during our lifetime when it is clear to us like daylight that God in heaven cares very deeply about us and we feel his closeness. During these times it is easy to tell the world about God's infinite kindness. However, there are times during our life when it is night, when our vision is unclear, where feel frightened and all alone. During these times, it is our faith that there is a brighter day, which must carry us through the difficult times. We use our memory of the times when we had clarity to give us direction and hope.

The Ramban (Nachmanides) writes an incredible parable to this. He said that it is similar to someone trying to walk through a forest at night during a thunderstorm. It is dark and scary and one cannot see where one is going. But every now and then, there is a flash of lightning! Suddenly, for an instant everything is illuminated and the person can see the path clearly. When it becomes dark again, the person then has to use the memory of the flash to give guidance through the forest.

In Judaism, we are constantly trying to achieve these goals. We have shown that in every moment; every act, whether eating, drinking or having sex is an opportunity to enrich our souls. Our mission is to find God underneath every stone and inside every crevice. Our goal is to keep searching for meaning and infuse every moment with infinite meaning. Our goal is to look at the beauty and oneness of God's creations and to give testimony to His awesome Name. Every moment we can transform the physical world into a world laden with spiritual power. This is the hidden path on which our lifelong journey takes place.

Spiritual Exercises

1. Try to think of an event in your life when you felt God's presence. What made you feel that way at that time? Can that feeling return in other circumstances as well?

2. Try to think of a place in nature that you once went to when you felt God's presence. What was special about that place?

3. Try to think of something you once read that made you think about God. What was special about that passage that you read? Can you find time to read other books that will bring back that feeling?

4. Try to set aside a few minutes each day to close your eyes and think about God. Then try to monitor how it starts to change your life.

Chapter 2
What it Means to Be a Jew

My nation is weak, its body is feeble.
Its spirit sways like a reed in the water,
But its inner soul is as strong as the Heavens.
I know its value, and the unique nature of its life.
It mocks all of its oppressors.
Even when it bows before them,
It recognizes its everlasting strength.
It recognizes that its enemies' strength
Is merely a passing shadow.
It is as mighty as a young lioness
Whose heart is inflamed.
It is as bold as a lioness
Fighting for its cubs.

~ Rabbi Abraham Isaac Kook

BEING JEWISH IS SPECIAL. God has given us a very unique role in world history, different than any other nation. In the very beginning of the Torah, God told Abraham to look at the heavens for one day his children will be as numerous as the stars of the sky, and as the sand by the sea. He bound a covenant with Abraham, stating that a great nation will one day arise from his seed.

Being chosen does not mean that we are better than other nations of the world. Every human being is given a unique soul that is part of the Divine. At the beginning of Genesis, God says, "Let us make man in God's image." This verse refers clearly to *all* men, for each of us contains the spark of the Divine. Genesis continues and says, "And God blew into his nostrils the soul of life; and man became a living soul." This verse uses the word *neshamah*, "soul" to describe the breath that God breathed into each and every one of us. This means every one of us has a part of God Himself inside of us. This was given to Adam, the first man to possess a Divine soul, long before the Jewish People came into existence.

Furthermore, the Talmud gives a startling insight into why God did not create more people originally and instead chose to create only one man and woman (Adam and Eve) from whom we all came from. This is to teach us no one can say they came from better ancestors and are therefore superior, since we all came from the same father and mother. Furthermore, Judaism has never preached that only we have a portion of Paradise at the exclusion of everyone else. The Talmud states in numerous places that the righteous gentiles of the earth have a share in Paradise as well. Additionally, the Torah commands us to universally love our fellow man as we love ourselves and to show kindness to the orphan and widow. The Torah does not specify to only show kindness to those who are Jewish; these verses are universal. Many of the greatest sages in the Talmud were close friends with the gentiles of the communities they lived in, and spoke highly of their wisdom. Wisdom can be found amongst all people as the *Pirkei Avot* (Ethics of our Fathers) declares, "Who is a wise person? One who can learn from *all* people." Our Sages further state that if someone declares there is wisdom among the nations of the world, that person should be believed.

So great is the importance to love everyone, whether Jewish or not Jewish, that Rabbi Abraham Isaac Kook writes that one is not living up to what Judaism is unless one feels this way. He writes, "The love for all people must be alive in heart and soul, a love for all people and a love for all nations, expressing itself a desire for the spiritual and material advancement; hatred may direct itself only to the evil and filth in the world. One cannot reach the exalted position of being able to recite the verse from the morning prayer, "Praise the Lord, invoke His name, declare His works among the nations" (1 Chron. 16:8), without experiencing the deep, inner love stirring one to a solicitousness for all nations, to improve their material state, to promote their happiness. This disposition qualifies the Jewish People to experience the spirit of the Messiah."

What it Means to Be Chosen

So what does it mean to be chosen? Chosen means that we are designated for a specific role. This role is taught to us by the Torah, namely the path of Monotheism and the values and standards of morality. The Bible teaches us the path we are to lead our lives. It educates us to the pitfalls of sexual immorality, murder, lying, and theft, as well as the importance of charity, kindness, and prayer. These traits were emulated by the Patriarchs, Matriarchs, and leaders of the Bible. Abraham taught the world about the Oneness of God, and the importance of loving kindness. Isaac represents the embodiment of Justice, and Jacob represented Truth. Joseph taught us that one can overcome temptations when he resisted the seductions of Potiphar's wife. The Bible even tells us when one can act zealous to preserve God's name, as Phinehas (*Pinchas*) did when he killed Zimri. The Bible even teaches us about the path to repentance, as King David atoned for his sin with Bathsheba. The greatness of the biblical characters is that they all had weakness and struggles and still were able to rise to the levels that they did. These are universal truths and being the People of the Book means we are to spread its messages.

God has even joined His name to His People. The Hebrew word *Yisrael* comes from *yisra El*, which means the "Officer of God." The very name by which are called shows that it is our mission to spread God's word. Alternatively, the word *Yisrael* may come from the word *yashor El*, which means "Straight to God," for we have the ability to develop a direct link to God. One of the reasons that the commentators give why the Jewish People were commanded to give half a shekel in the wilderness instead of a whole one is because God serves as our other half. He is what completes us as a people.

The Jerusalem Talmud writes something remarkable by way of analogy:

> God joined His name with Israel. To what can this be compared? To a king who had a small key to his palace. The king said, "If I leave the key as it is, then it will surely get lost. Rather, I will attach a chain to it, so that if it should get lost, the chain will still be on me." So too here, God said, "If I leave the Jewish People alone, they will eventually be lost among the nations. Instead, I will attach My name to them." What purpose will this serve? As Joshua prayed, "The Canaanite and all the inhabitants of the land

will hear and will surround us and cut off our name from the earth. What will You do for your Great Name" which is joined with us?

This parable is very deep and powerful, and has very broad ramifications. In this parable, we are the "key" to God's Palace, the world of the Spirit. The parable says that the key is small, and rightly so, for the Jewish People is small in number. The parable also speaks volumes to us, for it says that whenever a Jew feels lost, he can remember the great chain that is linked to our key, the Great Name that God has attached to us. Through remembering our name, Israel, we remember once again who we are, and once again feel reconnected.

Remembering Who We Are

Rabbi Nachman writes a similar idea when describing the special significance of Yom Kippur, the holiest day of the Jewish calendar. Rabbi Nachman writes to imagine a king who has a son who chooses to leave his father's home and forget his royal lineage. He decides to dress in ordinary civilian clothing and blend in with his surroundings. Much time goes by, and the prince seemed to forget who he once was. The king sends emissaries to convince the prince to return home, but the prince refuses to believe that there is anything extraordinary about him. Finally, a wise elder in the community says that he will be able to persuade the prince to return home. He asked the king to buy the most expensive telescope he can find and leave the curtains to the prince's room wide open. He then set out to look for the prince. When he found the prince, he once again told him that he was a special prince who held a unique place in a palace. When the prince did not believe him, he told him to look through his telescope.

When the prince saw his room, he remembered who he was. And so he returned home.

This is the message of Yom Kippur, the Day of Atonement. A Jew for one day looks into the telescope and sees who he really is. He remembers that he is a prince, and his Father is the King, and he has a special room inside of himself called the Soul which is in the palace of the King. He realizes how far he has distanced himself from his Father over the past year, and he yearns to once again strive to become closer. This is the path to repentance.

Along similar lines Rabbi Abraham Isaac Kook writes a remarkable idea about the holiday of Hanukkah. Hanukkah as we all know is the story when a small band of Jews called the Hasmoneans was able to drive the Greeks out of the Temple. The priests wanted to light the *Menorah* in the Temple as part of their service to God. However, they were not able to find a jar of oil that was pure, for they had all been defiled by the Greeks. Finally, after much searching, they were able to find one small jar that was pure and untouched, which still had the seal of the High Priest on it. Miraculously, this small jar burned for eight days, instead of the one day it was expected to burn.

What does this jar symbolize? What does it mean for us in modern day times? Rabbi Kook writes that this symbolizes that despite all of the impurities which surround us, there is deep within each of us a pure soul that has been untouched by the filth of the world, a soul which still has the seal of the High Priest engraved on it. When we find this "jar" within ourselves and we light it, God miraculously allows it to burn much longer than expected.

In the chapter on Chassidut, we will discuss the idea of recognizing that the real world is the world we don't see, the inner world, the world of the soul. While it is true that Chassidut emphasizes this idea more, in reality it is true of Judaism itself. We see this from the very origins of our people. Our father Abraham lived in a world of pagans, a world where the sun, the moon, and the stars were worshiped as deities. In the heathen mind, the gods had to be visible and corporeal. The idea of one God, and of a God that couldn't be seen in any way, was unheard of in its time. But something inside of Abraham told him this couldn't be true. The *Midrash* writes that at an exceptionally young age, Abraham looked at the world as a giant palace filled with light. Such a palace, he said, must surely have a builder. And so he began to explore, and study, and felt God's presence inside himself long before God actually spoke to him. Abraham is often called *ha-ivri*, "The Hebrew." However, there is something deeper it is hinting to. The Hebrew word *over*, related to *ivri*, can also mean "cross over." On a simple level this may mean the Abraham "crossed over" to the other side of the Jordan when he obeyed God to come to the Land of Canaan. However, the commentators explain this on a deeper level; that Abraham "crossed over" into uncharted territory, so to speak, that he decided to go against the grain of the world. He decided to believe in and follow what he knew in his heart, namely that there is One and only One true God in this world.

And so *Am Yisrael*, the Jewish People, was born. This would lead eventually to not only the beginning of our story as a people, but the story of two other major religions, Christianity and Islam, worshipped by over two billion people and spanning over two millennia.

The name *Yisrael* has even more significance. The Kabbalah teaches us that the name *Yisrael* actually is an acronym for our Patriarchs and Matriarchs according to the Hebrew spelling of their names. The first letter, *yud*, stands for *Yitzchak* (Isaac) and *Yaakov* (Jacob). The second letter, *sin*, stands for Sarah. The third letter, *resh*, stands for Rachel and Rebecca. The fourth letter, *aleph*, stands for Abraham. And finally, the last letter, *lamed*, stand for Leah.

This is an amazing teaching, but what does this mean? What was God trying to teach us by hiding the Patriarchs and Matriarchs in the name of our people? The answer is very simple. God was trying to help us understand that each one of us has inherited the great character traits of our Patriarchs and Matriarchs. It is part of our DNA. We have Abraham's unconditional loving kindness, Rachel's nurturing motherly capabilities, and Jacob's passion for Truth. This is indeed a great privilege and honor, but with it, also comes a great responsibility. The Jewish People have been given a task, and that is to teach the word of God to the world. The verse says we are to be an *or la-goyim*, a "light onto the nations." Many Jews unfortunately don't live up to their national task and act in a way that is not befitting of their Divine mission. These Jews have unfortunately not only brought shame to themselves, but also shame to God's great Name. However, many Jews have chosen to fulfill their lifelong duty in spreading God's message to the world.

The Tribulations of Being Jewish

This task has, sadly enough, brought us overwhelming hardship and suffering. The Torah has prophesied that we will be "a nation which will dwell alone." World history has proven this to be true. We are a small struggling nation that tries to survive among powerful and fierce enemies, a nation constantly forced to defend itself, and endure worldwide condemnation for doing so. No people have been more persecuted in the annals of human history, and yet endured it with dignity and grace. This is often because of our unique role in bringing morality and ethics to the world. Many of our enemies have even admitted to these truths. Adolf Hitler once said that we deserve to suffer, for the Jews "have brought circumcision to the body and conscience to the soul."

Ironically, instead of getting weaker by persecution and annihilation, we have only grown stronger. Torah Judaism today is thriving more now than ever before. In God's covenant to our People, he told Abraham his children will be "like the stars of the sky and like the sand of sea." Why this comparison? Why specifically are we compared to sand and to stars? The answer may be because sand is the one element of the earth that when it is burnt it doesn't disintegrate, but rather becomes stronger and is transformed into something more beautiful than it once was; namely glass. So too with stars, that when it is darkest outside, that is when they shine the most. So it is with the Jewish People. The blows we have had to endure throughout the centuries, both physically and spiritually have made us stronger and even more beautiful. This is not to say that we would ever want such beatings. It is only a testament to the eternity and wonder of our People.

Despite the relentless determination of our enemies, we have survived, and we always will survive. One Roman emperor once said to a Talmudic Sage, "Great is the Lamb, Israel, for it has survived amongst seventy wolves." The Sage replied, "Great is the Shepherd who rescues and protects her." Divine Providence will always ensure our survival. This is as we say in the Passover *Seder*, "In every generation, they will arise to annihilate us, but the Holy One Blessed Be He will save us from their hands." Not only have we survived, but often we shined the most when we were persecuted. The verse in Song of Songs, which is the love story between God and His people, says we are "a rose among the thorns." On a deeper level the Zohar says that just as roses emit their strongest fragrance when they are rubbed, so too the Jewish People reveal their strongest fragrance when they are persecuted.

The Extraordinary Influence of the Jewish People

What is also amazing is how much the Jewish People have contributed to the world at large. Our ranks have won an unprecedented number of Nobel prizes completely disproportionate to our tiny number. Israel, a tiny state surrounded by enemies from all sides, ranks among the top in the world in numerous areas, including medical research, military achievements, space advancement, and technological breakthroughs. While the great and mighty empires of history have come and gone, from Rome, to Greece, to Sparta, to Babylonia, to Viking, have remnants remaining only in the history books, statues, and museums, the Jew has not only outlived them all but has grown in stature and rank.

Our role in world history has also won the admiration of many. Many have even seen the Hidden Hand which has guided our people. Mark Twain wrote:

He is as prominent on the planet as any other people, and his commercial importance is extravagantly out of proportion to the smallness of his bulk. His contributions to the world's list of great names in literature, science, art, music, finance, medicine, and abstruse learning are also away out of proportion to the weakness of his numbers. He has made a marvelous fight in this world, in all the ages; and has done it with his hands tied behind him. He could be vain of himself, and be excused for it. The Egyptian, the Babylonian, and the Persian rose, filled the planet with sound and splendor, then faded to dream-stuff and passed away; the Greek and the Roman followed, and made a vast noise, and they are gone; other peoples have sprung up and held their torch high for a time, but it burned out, and they sit in twilight now, or have vanished. The Jew saw them all, beat them all, and is now what he always was, exhibiting no decadence, no infirmities of age, no weakening of his parts, no slowing of his energies, no dulling of his alert and aggressive mind. All things are mortal but the Jew; all other forces pass, but he remains. What is the secret of his immortality?

The Jew can live either in this world or above it. This is why the newborn boy is circumcised on the eighth day, for eight is the number that is above the physical world. The world was created in "seven days," but the baby is circumcised on the eight day. This is also why the Hanukkah candles burned for eight days. It is also why the High Priest wears eight vestments on Yom Kippur when he enters the Holy of Holies to commune with God on Yom Kippur. When a Jew connects to the Divine, he or she is linking to the supernatural. We find this idea in the name of our forefather Isaac. Isaac was the first born Jew in the world, and he was named this because the word *Yitzchak* means "he laughs." This is because Abraham and Sarah laughed when they learned Sarah conceived, for she was in her eighties at the time and completely barren. The *Midrash* even says that she did not even have the organs needed for procreation. So Sarah laughed at the incredibility of the situation. Why was it so important for him to receive this name? Couldn't they find a more inspiring name? Rabbi Akiva Tatz writes that he was given this name precisely for this reason. The Jew comes from supernatural beginnings; his very origin and survival are miraculous. Indeed, it is an occasion for laughter, for it is impossible to believe.

It is interesting to note that when discussing the Binding of Isaac, the verse talks of *afaro shel Yitzchak*, "the ashes of Isaac," as if he was in fact sacrificed! What does this mean? Abraham was certainly willing to sacrifice his beloved child as he was commanded to by God, but we all know he was stopped at the very last instant! What does this mean? Rabbi Binny Freedman gave a most startling answer; that on a deeper more mystical level Isaac *was* in fact sacrificed on the altar! On the one hand, Isaac remained alive and very much here in this world, and on the other hand his soul ascended to Heaven on the altar. An amazing idea, the Jew lives with one foot in this world, and one foot in the next world. One part of us is still very much in the here and now, and one part of us is offered up to Heaven.

We have seen our extraordinary nature in modern times as well. Our People endured the Nazi Holocaust in Europe; some six million people were murdered, the largest genocide in human history. But what occurred only a few years later? Then came the miraculous birth of the State of Israel; a triumphant return to our biblical homeland after two thousand years. We have risen from the ashes, a resurrection quite like no other nation in history, a history that is replete with wonders which border on the sublime.

We have the ability today to experience God's love, even when we live in distant lands, dispersed among the nations of the world. The Zohar compares us to a prince who lives in an area that is surrounded by tanneries. God looks past the unpleasant odor of the tannery and seeks out his beloved people, Israel.

The Torah has also said we are "treasured people." Elsewhere it says of us "A kingdom of priests and a holy people." Admired by many and scorned by many. Exalted and honored, and yet broken and desolate. This has always been our destiny. With each day we continue to strive to teach the world about the God we know and love. Our mission began with our Forefather Abraham and will be completed when the Messiah arrives.

Spiritual Exercises

1. Try to think of a moment when you felt totally connected to the Jewish People. What was it that you felt connected you so deeply?

2. Try to think of a Jew in your personal life that totally inspires you, and makes you feel proud to be Jewish. What makes you inspired about that person? Try to think of ways you can emulate that person.

3. Try to think of a famous Jewish personality that totally inspires you and makes you feel proud to be Jewish. What makes you inspired about that person? Try to think of ways you can emulate that person.

4. Try to think of a Jewish institution you love and feel passionate about. Try to think of ways you can help support that institution, either physically, emotionally, spiritually, or financially.

Chapter 3
Healthy Body, Healthy Soul

Great is our physical demand. We need a healthy body. We dealt much with soulfulness; we forgot the holiness of the body. We neglected the physical health and strength; we forgot that we have holy flesh; no less than holy spirit... Our repentance will succeed only if it will be—with all its splendid spirituality—also a physical return, which produces healthy blood, healthy flesh, mighty solid bodies, a fiery spirit radiating over powerful muscles.

~ Rabbi Abraham Isaac Kook

I HAVE ALWAYS STRUGGLED WITH my health and weight. Thank God, not in a major way. I have overall been blessed with a pretty healthy body and never put on weight to the point of obesity. But nonetheless, both have always been struggles for me throughout my life. I was a little chubby in high school, but then ballooned out, like so many others my year in Israel. It was there in Israel I met what would become my two best friends throughout the year, namely falafel and shwarma. Shwarma is meat made in such a greasy way that I believe one portion has enough oil to light your *menorah* for eight days (perhaps longer!). It's hard to imagine living on that stuff for a whole year, but that was pretty much it, with of course several cups of coffee thrown in. I knew I put on weight, but didn't realize how much, until I went home to visit my family for Passover, and the first comment they said when I stepped off the plane was something like, "Wow, Yisroel! At least we know you weren't starving when you were there!" My sister said, "Yisroel, is that really you? Or do you have a pillow hiding under your shirt?" My American friends were even more cynical, "Yisroel! Wow, I didn't know you were pregnant! And from the looks of it, it seems you are expecting twins!" The jokes went on and on, and of course the message was driven home that it was time to hit the treadmill.

And hit the treadmill I did, but in an even better way. I went for a run every night through the streets of Jerusalem after Passover, and even somehow managed to cut back on the junk food I was eating for so long, and the weight managed to come off. By the time I came home at the end of the year, I was skinnier than I had been in a long time, even before high school.

I have had struggles with overall health as well. I have always had digestive problems and have suffered from migraine headaches. The struggles still continue to this day. These struggles are not unique to me of course; nearly everyone I know struggles with weight and overall health issues. And this struggle is at the forefront of the American consciousness today. Some surveys show that over 35% of American adults are obese, and that number is expected to continue to grow. We live in what I call the Popcorn Movie Generation. No other generation has lived such a sedentary lifestyle, created to some degree by the conveniences of modern technology and the availability of media entertainment. This is a hole that unfortunately many of us have created for ourselves.

We all have at some point heard the phrase, "You are what you eat." Whatever we take into our bodies becomes a part of who we are. This doesn't just apply to food, but other actions can impact our health as well, like smoking, substance abuse, and excessive alcohol. Our physical activity becomes a part of who we are as well. The exercise we do, or lack thereof, will determine the state our bodies will be in.

The Jewish Perspective on Health

From a Jewish perspective, does all of this have any bearing on us? Is there any correlation between our physical health and our spiritual lives? And what are the Torah's views on eating healthy and living a healthy lifestyle?

To begin to find the answers means of course looking into the Torah itself. The Torah commands us *ve-nishmartem me'od le-nafshoteichem*, "you shall surely protect your bodies." This is the main source for the precept to preserve our health in every way possible. Furthermore, the Torah forbids us to harm ourselves in any way, and to save a life one can transgress nearly every law in the Torah. One may even violate the Sabbath and eat pig if it will cause a life to be saved, including one's own. God, as we know, is the ultimate healer, as it is written in the verse, "I am the Lord, Your Healer." Through preserving our bodies as best as we can, we are, in a way emulating God. Emulating God, as discussed in the previous chapters, is one of the greatest ways to come close to Him. As it is written, "You shall walk in His ways."

The Body as a Sanctuary

The Talmud in one place regards the human body as a sanctuary. This idea always resonated deep within me about the importance of treating our bodies not only with dignity, but with care, the way one would a sanctuary. For this is the vessel we were given to bring ourselves closer to Him, and to reach our potential in this world.

This is why I believe the Talmud puts such an emphasis not only on health, but on cleanliness as well. The Talmud states that no tannery, grave, or carcass may be placed within fifty cubits (about eighty feet) of a human dwelling, and stressed that streets and market areas must be kept clean. The Sages declared it forbidden for a scholar to reside in a city that did not contain a public bath.

One of my favorite anecdotes in the Talmud came from the great sage Hillel. Once when Hillel was leaving his disciples, they said to him, "Master, where are you going?" He replied, "To do a pious deed." They asked, "What may that be?" He replied: "To take a bath." They asked, "Is that a pious deed?" He replied, "Yes. If in the theaters and circuses, the images of the king must be kept clean by the man to whom they have been entrusted, how much more is it a duty of man to care for the body, since man has been created in the divine image and likeness." Thus we see preserving our bodies takes on an even more special role since it is acknowledging the Divine Image inside of us.

In medieval times, no rabbi practiced as well as wrote extensively about this as the great Maimonides. Maimonides, as we know, was the royal physician of the Sultan of Egypt. He didn't just believe maintaining one's health was only a moral imperative, but it was also a *halachic* imperative, that we were obligated according to Jewish Law to preserve our health. He writes in his *Mishneh Torah*, the Code of Jewish Law, "Since maintaining a healthy and sound body is among the ways of God—for one cannot understand or have any knowledge of the Creator if he is ill—therefore he must avoid that which harms the body and accustom himself to that which is helpful and helps the body become stronger." Maimonides believed that a physician demonstrates greater skill by *preventing* illness than he does by *curing* illness.

In modern times, Rabbi Abraham Isaac Kook wrote extensively about the importance of physical health as a prerequisite to *teshuvah* (repentance). At the time Rabbi Kook felt that every *yeshivah* should have exercise equipment as well as an area to play sports. At the time, Rabbi Kook received tremendous backlash, for he was seen as being too liberal, and he was accused of taking *yeshivah* students away from Torah study. Only now do we see the truth to Rabbi Kook's ideas, for nearly every *yeshivah* has space for exercise and sports.

Correlations Between the Body and the Soul

I have always been fascinated by the many correlations between the mind and the body. One of the most well-known books on the subject was John Sarno's *The Mind-Body Connection*, which deals with understanding that chronic pain, especially back pain, can be controlled almost completely through psychological techniques. Sarno himself has treated and cured countless number of people through his techniques. Some studies on meditation have shown that meditation not only has numerous psychological benefits, but physiological benefits as well. Studies have shown that it can help reduce blood pressure and other heart conditions, as well as curb appetite and therefore assist in weight loss.

Perhaps even more compelling is the effect our bodies have on our spiritual lives. I have seen many students in *yeshivah* who began studying Torah better once they started eating healthier and exercising more regularly. I have seen a similar correlation in my own personal life. The times when I was eating healthy and exercising, I felt more spiritually alive and therefore my Torah study and prayer became more meaningful and enriching. The times when I was eating poorly and not exercising I felt spiritually dull and lifeless. There have been many testimonials of people who talked about the many added spiritual benefits of weight loss as well. I remember reading about Steve Vaught, an obese individual who fell into a horrible state of depression after accidentally killing someone in a car accident. He decided to walk across America to lose weight and regain his self-esteem. Not only did he lose about a hundred pounds, but felt less depressed and more spiritual as a result of his journey.

There are several reasons why it is so important to stay healthy from a spiritual perspective. The main reason is the very close relationship between not only the *mind* and body, but the *soul* and body as well. The body and soul are totally entwined. This means that each needs the other in order to accomplish its purpose in this world, as described in one of the most beautiful parables in the entire Talmud:

> [The Roman Emperor] Antoninus said to Rabbi [Judah the Prince], "The body and soul could exonerate themselves from judgment. How is this so? The body says, 'The soul sinned, for from the day that it separated from me, lo, I am like a silent stone in the grave (without sinning)!' And the soul says, 'The body is the sinner, for from the day that I separated from it, lo, I fly in the air like a bird (without

sinning).'" He answered him, "I will tell you a parable. To what is the matter likened? To a king of flesh and blood who had a beautiful orchard and there were in it lovely ripe fruit, and he placed two guardians over it, one a cripple and the other blind. The cripple said to the blind man, 'I see beautiful ripe fruit in the orchard. Come and carry me and we will bring and eat them.' The cripple rode on the back of the blind man and they brought and ate them. After a while the owner of the orchard came and said to them, 'Where is my lovely fruit?' The cripple answered, 'Do I have legs to go?' The blind man answered, 'Do I have eyes to see?' What did he [the owner of the orchard] do? He placed the cripple on the back of the blind man and judged them as one. So also the Holy One, Blessed be He, brings the soul and throws it into the body and judges them as one." This is at is written in Psalms, "He shall call to the Heavens above and the earth below to judge his people." He shall call to the Heavens above" refers to the soul, "and the earth below" refers to the body.

Here we see the dual partnership between the body and soul in this world. But this isn't just a relationship for negative behavior; it is a relationship for positive behavior as well. This means in order to develop a relationship with God in a positive way, we must need both the partnership between the body and soul for nearly all the *mitzvot* require both the body and soul. When the body is weakened, it becomes more difficult to perform *mitzvot*, and one becomes more pre-occupied with health and less focused on developing a relationship with God. However, as one maintains his or her optimal health, performing the *mitzvot* is significantly easier and one has more ease in their daily living and peace of mind to develop a more intimate relationship with God. Eating right and exercising provides us with the necessary energy to be able to accomplish what we need to accomplish each day in our spiritual lives.

Over a century ago, Rabbi Samson Raphael Hirsch wrote similarly about the need to maintain one's health as vital to our service and relationship to God. When explaining the verse in Deuteronomy, "Take heed to yourself and take care of yourself," Rabbi Hirsch writes, "You may not… in any way weaken your health or shorten your life. Only if the body is healthy is it an efficient instrument for the spirit's activity.... Therefore you should avoid everything which might possibly injure your health…. And the law asks you to be even more circumspect in avoiding danger to life and limb than in the avoidance of other transgressions."

But there is another reason why diet especially plays an important role in our spiritual lives. Perhaps more than anything, it builds discipline and character, and prevents us from becoming self-indulgent beings focused only on gratifying our physical desires whenever we want to. By controlling our diet, *we* are controlling our bodies and not allowing our bodies to control *us*. This is a re-alignment of priorities which takes a lot of hard work but leads us to develop ourselves more spiritually.

Making Changes in Our Lifestyle

All of us deep down know the importance of this concept, and at times many of us make the resolve to change our daily eating and exercise habits. The problem is that often our resolve fades away when the next custard donut comes our way. (Dunkin Donuts has always been one of my weak spots.) The key to re-instating our resolve, I believe, is always to think about our end goals during those moments.

We all want to have the best bodies physically since we know it will help give us the energy and confidence we need to accomplish both our physical and spiritual goals. Once again, I believe maintain the mental image of where we want to be can help us achieve what we want.

There are many worthwhile books that have been published on how to manage a balanced diet, whether your personal goal is to lose weight or maintain a healthy lifestyle. There are many exercise regimens available, from the novice to the most advanced, which are highly instructive about how to lose weight, get toned, or build muscle.

As a general rule, most of us can reduce the amount of needless calories we consume. There are many "invisible calories" that we often don't realize we consume throughout the day, but can have great impact on our weight and overall health. Some guidelines may be:

- switching from whole milk to skim milk (this goes for milk in cereal and coffee, too),

- switching from sugary to low-calorie cereals for breakfast,

- reducing caffeine intake, and avoid adding sugar or artificial sweeteners to coffee (also avoid sugary caffeinated beverages),

- switching from bleached flour to whole-grain carbohydrates, like whole-wheat bread, brown rice, and whole-wheat pasta, but remember that even whole-grain foods contain calories,

- avoiding high-calorie topping on pasta, like butter, margarine, and cheese, as well as high-calorie salad dressings, which often contain more fat than an unhealthy meal,

- drinking eight glasses of water a day, switching from soft drinks (regular and diet) to seltzer or water,

- being careful about snacks, as an otherwise healthy diet can be compromised by excessive snacking; try to have fruits and vegetables as snacks instead of junk food; for example, apples, oranges, grapes, blueberries, baby carrots, cucumbers, and spinach leaves, and avoid nuts, which are high-calorie; another alternative is naturally popped popcorn without butter or margarine added,

- trying to calorie-count each meal and keep a personal log. Most people should not consume more than 2,000 to 2,500 calories each day,

- avoiding products fried in oil, and eating foods that are baked or cooked in water,

- avoiding processed foods, which often have extra calories dumped in that you don't need,

- switching from red meat to poultry and low-fat fish (keeping in mind that not all fish is low-fat),

- setting aside time each week to exercise; consult your physician about how often you should exercise and what exercises you should do (your doctor will be proud of you just for asking!), but studies show that for many people, elevating the heart-rate for thirty to forty-five minutes several times a week has the same effect as taking an anti-depressant, which shows how physical health helps the mind, body, and soul as well,

- going to a yoga class once a week, if you have the time, since the stretches it teaches increase flexibility, and they also teach how to reduce stress (which can lower blood pressure), and help achieve inner peace and harmony.

Notice how the last two directly impact physical health as well as psychological and spiritual health. Remember, however, that this list is only a series of suggestions and recommendations that have worked for many, but may not apply to everyone. Please consult a physician if you are planning to make any major changes to your diet or exercise regimen so he can guide you further. Overall, this list affirms the mantra we can live by, "DO NOT LIVE TO EAT, BUT EAT TO LIVE!" My blessing to everyone is to live healthy and thereby further reach our potential in this world, which in turn can lead to a happier and more meaningful life.

Spiritual Exercises

1. Try to remember a time when you were eating right and exercising regularly. How did you feel at the time physiologically? Psychologically? Spiritually?

2. Try to remember a time in your life when you were not eating right and not exercising regularly. How did you feel at the time physiologically? Psychologically? Spiritually?

3. Speak to your physician about the physiological, psychological, and even spiritual benefits of eating right, and find something that works for you and that you can commit to following. Then document each day how the new diet and exercise plan is changing both your day and your life.

Chapter 4
A Deeper Look at Suffering

*Anyone who has ever built anywhere a new heaven
first found the power thereto in his own hell.*

~ Friedrich Nietzsche

SUFFERING IS THE GREATEST QUESTION to plague man from the dawn of time till the present day. Philosophers have struggled with it, scholars have scoured through countless number of texts in the hope of finding answers, and countless numbers of books have been written on the subject. And most importantly, all of us, the common man, who trudges on each day through the often bleak landscapes that encompass our days, mystifies us, and often gnaws at our beliefs and faith. The question, of course, is the Great Question of Suffering. Not only why there *is* suffering, but even bigger, why does God allow it to occur, and often at times in nature, He even seems to *instigate* the suffering, to take an active role in bringing the suffering to *us*. It is the question on every parent's lips who has buried their child, on every hospital bed when the doctor comes back with the test results and murmurs the fateful diagnosis, and when the phone call comes about the friend who was hit by the car, the list goes on and on. It is the question of, "Why?"

Ever since we were little children, we are taught of God's love for us, how He cares for each of us, and how everything He does is for our good. Furthermore, we are taught, and even *commanded* in the Torah, "You shall love the Lord our God with all of our hearts and all of our souls." How are we to understand this? How can we believe in a loving God when so much of what we see is to the contrary? And how could we possibly love Him, when often all what we see is betrayal? Isn't the greatest form of betrayal to love when someone who we think "loves" us intentionally hurts us?

The question is even stronger on a Jewish level, when we are taught we are God's chosen, his "treasured people" and yet history has shown anything *but* that. How many Jews have been maimed or killed in invasions in biblical times, persecutions and pogroms in the middle ages, and terrorist attacks that continue to this very day?

The question was at its strongest when over sixty years ago, the Jewish world was shattered with a catastrophe far greater than its long and torturous history had ever endured. More than six million Jews, including over one and a half million children were butchered like animals through nearly every type of suffering imaginable, gas chamber, starvation, bullets, disease, medical experiments, and more, all at the hands of a brutal dictator and his gang of thugs. Over two thirds of European Jewry and a third of our people perished in the Nazi Holocaust of Europe. No movie, no memorial service, and even no first hand testimonial can quite convey the horror that our people endured, when the verse in Deuteronomy, "I will hide My face from you" was fulfilled to a degree we never thought was imaginable.

In my career as a physical therapist I have seen with my own eyes pain on so many levels throughout the human life cycle, from childhood to adulthood, to mature adulthood.

I have seen the entire gamut of the experience of suffering, from disability, to injury, to physical illness, to mental illness. I have held the hands of hospice patients in their final days. I have stood next to young once healthy people who had a spinal cord injury or traumatic brain injury. I have worked with children who have never known what it is to walk on their own two feet. I have seen cancer patients, dementia patients, stroke patients, the list never ends. I have heard their soft weeping as I walked past their rooms in the nursing facilities.

On a personal level, the subject has troubled me a great deal. I have had more than my share of difficulties, especially in the area of relationships. I had been single and lonely for many years before finding the special person to share my life with. During those years, watching all of my friends get married and start families all around me left me wondering if it would ever happen to me, if I would spend the rest of my life wandering this earth all by myself, with no wife and no children to come home to. I remember once being particularly crushed when a girl I was convinced was my soul mate broke up with me. I tried everything, from drowning myself in a sea of anti-depressants, to therapy, to trying to jump into the usual fruitless rebound relationships. But even more than the hurt and loneliness was the feeling of being abandoned by God. I cried to Him all of the time to help me, but the years continued to slip by. I struggled with it, how could a God I believed (or at least was *supposed* to believe was a loving caring God) seem to ignore the cries of one of His children?

One of the most common answers for explaining human suffering is to say it is to atone for our sins in this world so we may attain a portion in the World to Come. To a certain extent, this answer is true. Indeed, there is a well-known concept in the Talmud of *yissurin shel ahavah*, "afflictions of love." This means that God often allows us to suffer out of His love for us, so we may get a larger eternal reward in the Next World. The Talmud even says that the World to Come is one of three things that only comes through suffering (the other two are Torah and the Land of Israel).

To a certain extent, I feel that although this all may be true, it still does not answer the question of human suffering fully. I don't feel in this world we will ever fully understand it. The Talmud even writes that it is not for us to explain the suffering of the righteous and the tranquility of the wicked. This is because I believe we don't know the answer, and anyone who claims to know the answer is either misguided or lying. Moses, the greatest prophet who ever lived, struggled with this question, when he asked God to be able to see Him, which the commentators explain means to see and understand His ways. God answered him He would only show Moses His back, which the commentators explain means when we reach the next world, often called the World of Truth, we will understand His ways. But in this world He says, "No one can see me and live."

So for those who have tried to answer the question of suffering, more often than not, the answers seems trivial, shallow, and forced, and generally the question remains much stronger than the answer. So this chapter does not attempt to answer the question directly, more to give an approach to help us deal with suffering in general.

Of all the great Chassidic Masters, perhaps no one wrote more about human emotion than Rabbi Nachman of Breslov. We are told little of his life, except that he endured much suffering. He lost all three of his children at a young age, and was thus one of the only Chassidic leaders without a successor. He lived in poverty for most of his life, and died at thirty-eight of tuberculosis. Often he was ridiculed by many of the other Masters, and was not truly appreciated for his greatness during his lifetime. Like many spiritual giants, he was years ahead of his generation, and therefore was not understood until years after his soul had already left this world.

Rabbi Nachman wrote extensively about melancholy as he himself experienced it. He often told his faithful student Rabbi Nathan Sternhartz that he felt every day as if in a dream that he had reached the lowest possible place on earth, only to awaken and realize he had fallen to an even lower place. At times nothing could give him solace, not even Torah study, prayer, or meditation. He spent long periods of time in isolation, and did not even want to be visited by his most faithful.

And yet more than any other Rebbe, he writes about the importance of being happy. He would often say that it a great *mitzvah* to always be happy. He wrote that depression is the evil inclination, for it puts *kelipot,* husks that separate us from getting close to God, over us. He wrote some of the most inspiring quotes about the human struggle, and quotes that have endured to this day.

"There is nothing more whole than a broken heart."

"The whole entire world is a very narrow bridge, and the main thing is to have no fear."

"If you believe you can break, believe you can fix."

Somehow, Rabbi Nachman understood that somehow depression was a necessary vehicle in the service of God. How?

Suffering as a Precursor for Redemption

In the creation of the world, we find a very peculiar theme that remains unique to Judaism. We find in the book of Genesis by each day of creation that night precedes day, as it is written, "and it was evening, and it was morning, it was one day." This concept must be of utmost importance, since the Torah the opening paragraph in the Torah contains this verse. In Jewish Law, the day really begins at night, as the Sabbath begins at nightfall, as well as all of the other holidays. How are we to understand this? And what lesson can be learned from this?

Here we come to one of the most fundamental and deepest concepts in Judaism, for each day is a microcosm of our lives. The Torah essentially is teaching that *in order to reach the light we must first experience darkness.* This means that evil, pain, and sadness are not separate from good and happiness, but are a prerequisite to reach the state of joy we all so desperately want to attain. One can only experience true joy after one has been in a place of suffering. It is only in suffering that one does true contemplation and soul-searching, and only then can the person be ready to receive goodness.

This idea occurs countless times throughout the Torah. Joseph had to first be sold as a slave to a caravan of Ishmaelites and later thrown into prison before he was able to rise to the level of viceroy of Egypt. The Jewish People had to first be enslaved in Egypt before they could be forged into a People with the awesome revelations at Mount Sinai.

This idea even occurs in the modern day Jewish history. Right after experiencing the horrors of the Nazi Holocaust in Europe we experienced the birth of the State of Israel. Overnight, a despondent battered people who had walked through the furnace were able to once again returned home. A People who had just experienced the worst tragedy they had ever felt in the last two thousand years suddenly felt their greatest triumph.

This is why legend tells us that the Messiah will be born on Tisha B'Av. Tisha B'Av, the saddest day of the Jewish calendar, is the very same day that will one day bring us our Redeemer. When we are in the lowest place is when we begin to blossom.

One of my favorite passages in the Talmud illustrates this idea with the following story. Once, Rabbi Gamliel, Rabbi Elazar ben Azariah, Rabbi Joshua and Rabbi Akiva were ascending to Jerusalem. When they reached Mt. Scopus, they rent their clothing. When they arrived at the Temple mount, they saw a fox leaving from the Holy of Holies and Rabbi Akiva's friends began to cry. But Rabbi Akiva laughed. They asked him, "Why are you laughing?" He said to them, "Why are you crying?" They answered him, "Concerning this holy place, it says, 'And a stranger who approaches it [the Holy of Holies] will surely die' (Numbers 1). And now we see its defilement, as prophesied 'Foxes walked therein' (Lamentations 5:18). How could we not cry?" Rabbi Akiva replied that since he has witnessed the fulfillment of Uriah's prophecy of destruction, "Zion will ploughed like a field," (Micah 3), he became certain that Zechariah's redemptive prophecy would also be fulfilled, "The elder men and elder women will yet sit in the streets of Jerusalem." Rabbi Akiva's friends replied, "Akiva, you have comforted us, Akiva you have comforted us." The Sage Rabbi Akiva was able to see that within the destruction, one can see the seeds of redemption as well.

What can we learn from suffering? Rabbi Nachman quotes the verse in Psalms, "Happy is the man whom God chastises and from Your Torah you teach him." He explains that suffering is what brings the person to greater Torah insight. Perhaps it because at that moment he is experiencing his emotions in a very intense way; and Torah insights come in intense emotional state.

It is written in the Book of Deuteronomy, "I will conceal my face from you." This is a dark verse, for it speaks of a time when God will obscure His Face and not allow His Hand to be shown to the world. Some modern day commentators say that this verse is a reference to the

Holocaust, when God's Presence was hidden. However, the very next verse is, "And now you shall write for yourselves this song." How are we to understand this juxtaposition? Right after a verse about suffering, we have a verse about *singing*? However with this understanding, the passage is illuminated, for right after tragedy, there will be triumph, for this has been the story of our People throughout the millennia. After every night, the dawn will come, and once again, our People will sing.

Suffering as a Catalyst for Inspiration

Is it possible to gain insight, and even inspiration during difficult times? Most certainly, the answer is, emphatically, yes. It is for this reason that King David wrote some of his most poignant Psalms when he was running for his life from his own son Absalom. This is why Rabbi Shneur Zalman of Liadi was able to write much of his magnum opus *Tanya* while he sat in a Soviet prison. The Babylonian Talmud was written in the cold harshness of the Babylonian exile. The Talmud writes that the verse "And darkness surrounded me" refers to the Babylonian Talmud. Even in modern times, Rabbi Klonymous Kalman Shapira wrote the *Aish Kodesh* ("Holy Fire") while he watched his whole world crumble around him in the Warsaw Ghetto by the Nazis. It is said that the Modzitzer Rebbe composed of his most beautiful pieces of music while he was getting surgery without anesthesia. The list goes on and on.

However, a word of caution at this point is necessary. This does not mean we should ask to be tested in any way. For we are taught in the Talmud never ask for a test, because often we will fail. King David once asked for his faith and his inclinations to be tested, and he was warned he would surely fail. But he wanted a test nonetheless, and indeed he failed. He was tested with Bathsheba, and he succumbed to his desires. There are many commentators who explain that King David's sin is not as straightforward as it seems, but still on some level he committed a great wrongdoing. In fact the word *nissayon*, "test" or "trial," is very similar to the word *nes*, means "miracle." It is a great miracle to be able to pass a great test that God puts in our way. A person by nature cannot pass a test that is put his or her way, it takes a tremendous amount of self-control, introspection, and prayer, and only then, miraculously, can one overcome the challenge.

There is a very enigmatic passage in the Talmud which further alludes to this idea. It is written at the end of this life a *tzaddik* (righteous person) sees the evil inclination, and it appears to him or her like a giant insurmountable mountain. A *rasha* (evil person) on the other hand, sees the evil inclination, and it appears as a small flimsy speck of dust or hair that even a light wind can knock over. On the surface level, this passage seems to make no sense since shouldn't it be the opposite? Shouldn't a righteous person, who spent his or her entire life overcoming the challenges put forth by the evil inclination, shouldn't he now have the experience and strength to easily overcome the evil inclination? And since the wicked person spent his or her entire life chasing after every temptation, shouldn't the evil inclination seem to be an insurmountable mountain?

The answer hints at this concept we are discussing. The Evil Inclination is presented as how it actually *is* during one's lifetime; rather it is presented as *how it could be.* Meaning it is not referring to the *actual* power of the Evil Inclination one feels during one's lifetime, but rather the *potential* power that the Evil Inclination has. For a righteous person, who spent their life avoiding tempting situations, they now see just how strong the Evil Inclination could be, if one were to put oneself in a difficult situation. It indeed can seem to be an insurmountable mountain. However to a wicked person, who spent his or her life chasing the Evil Inclination, now sees it was all a façade, it was just a speck of dust that could be easily knocked over. Here we see the potential power of this Inclination, how if we were to ask to be put in a difficult situation and indeed if our wishes were granted, we could be faced with what seems to be an insurmountable mountain, or roadblock for our spiritual growth; how easy it is to fall during those challenges.

God Is With Us During Challenges

So even though we are not supposed to ask for tests, there is no question that difficult times can be times of tremendous inspiration. As difficult as it may sound to hear, God is *always* with us, even in the most difficult times. One of my favorite ideas was said by Rabbi Yisrael of Rizhin, while he was in prison for the crime of being Jewish. He expounded the well-known verse in Psalms, "As I walk through the valley of the shadow of death, I will have no fear, fear, because I know you are with me." Why is there a repetition of the word "fear"? He explains beautifully; I *should* not be afraid, but yet why am I still afraid? Because I know you *are with me,* because you are right here beside me, experiencing just what I am experiencing. It is also written in the verses, "I am with you in suffering." God is always right next to us, and experiencing our pain together with us.

There is an enigmatic passage in the Talmud which I believe alludes to this. The Talmud discusses a verse which says, "And if you do not heed this, My Spirit will cry in hidden chambers because of your haughtiness." The Talmud asks, does God really weep? But isn't it also written "Glory and Majesty are before Him, might and delight are in His place?" The Talmud gives the most cryptic answer; one verse is referring to His outer chamber, and one verse refers to His inner chamber. How are we to understand this? What is His outer chamber and what is His inner chamber? I believe that the answer can be that our outer world is the world that we see; the world where it seems God is always joyful even during difficult times. What is his inner chamber? His inner chamber is that which we don't see, his inner chamber is inside of each and every one of us. His inner chamber is deep within us, it is our soul. Inside He is with us, every step of the way, feeling our pain and weeping together with us. Often, as we discussed in the chapter on Chassidut, we know that what is most real is what we don't see. It is I believe the reason why so many have gained so much inspiration and closeness to God during these times, because it is specifically during those times that we feel God pulsating within us. So can we gain any insight into our suffering? Yes we definitely can, even as we don't understand why we need to experience it.

I think of it as a child who is separated from his parents. The child doesn't see the parents and at times may think he is abandoned, but the reality of it is the parents are feeling the pain of their missing child every day. It just is not in front of the child to see.

I was tormented a great deal when it came to writing this chapter, because more than any other chapter I knew this chapter would be the most personal for me. While much of this book has been discussing philosophical ideas, this chapter more than any of the others is for me a memoir. I have known pain, pain in the form of a loneliness that haunted me for many years. Each of us has our own daily struggles, and mine came in the form of spending frustrating years in search of my soul mate. Watching every friend of mine get married and have children, as I still struggled to even have a good first date, and coming home each night to an empty apartment. And as a physical therapist who worked with pre-school children, I longed so desperately to have children of my own, but could not seem to make any relationships work, a necessary prerequisite for marriage and having children.

And all the while I felt totally abandoned by God, and in turn wanted to abandon Him. But the ironic thing is that I knew I could never abandon God because He is all we have. And with each painful experience, afterward I realized how close He was during those times, and many of my most heartfelt songs and paintings during those times. Each time afterward I felt His embrace even stronger than ever before.

This concept, while certainly not an answer, can still help us have a greater understanding of suffering. Suffering, among other things, can create inside of us a longing. This is especially true during a time of great fear. There is a well known expression, "There is no atheist in a foxhole." How true this statement is! It is only in the potential absence of something that we come to appreciate it the most. Our heart beats an estimated two billion times in our lifetime; it is inside of us every moment, and yet we only *think* about our heart during a heart attack, when we are in danger of losing it, of our heart giving out. So too, only when we are in danger of *losing our souls,* during war or fatal illness, do we begin to think about how deeply our soul means to us, and begin to turn to the One who created our souls. Only then do we feel God's Presence in a more palpable way then we have ever felt.

This does not mean we cannot experience God in a very real way when we are not suffering. We all know of many people who have never tasted real suffering, and yet rose to extraordinary spiritual heights. However, suffering *forces* us to experience God, it forces us to come to terms with our own mortality, and our own dependence on Him.

And perhaps equally as important as the opportunity to develop a deeper relationship to God is the opportunity to develop our own personal growth. Going through a difficult experience is a chance to do serious introspection on our lives, our goals, and the time we spend here in this world. However, others grow bitter and angry at the world. I had seen this several times when I was working in hospitals and nursing homes as a physical therapist. Patients who were suffering generally had one of several reactions, either melancholy, rage, or a time to re-evaluate one's life and life decisions. People who see it as an opportunity for self-growth are often able to reach extraordinary heights that they wouldn't otherwise be able to achieve.

Inspiring People Who Have Suffered

In the celebrity world, one person I admired greatly was actor Christopher Reeve. Reeve, who was best known for playing Superman in the movies, was an actor who seemed to have it all. He was handsome, well-built, famous, wealthy, married to a beautiful woman and with beautiful kids. Then, in an instant, everything changed. While horseback riding, he fell of his horse, broke his neck, and had a C-1 level injury to his cervical spine, the worst possible spinal cord injury. He lost nearly all physical function, his arms and legs were paralyzed, and breathing became impossible without a respirator. Even speaking became extremely difficult; he was only able to speak in a whisper and only several words at a time. In the beginning, he contemplated suicide, and even thought of paying someone to end the suffering that had become his life. But through much therapy, support groups, and the love of his family, he was able to regain the strength to go on. Much can be said about the love his wife Donna continued to have for him, as was discussed in the chapter about love. But Christopher

Reeve went way beyond just having the will to live. He began to see the incredible potential he had to give others strength who were going through similar experiences. He began travelling all over the world, as difficult as that must have been in his situation and lectured everywhere to other people with spinal cord injuries. He also raised awareness in the media for people with spinal cord injury, as well as starting The Christopher Reeve Foundation, a charity to help fund medical research in the field as well as improve quality of life from those who suffered from this injury. He even produced and acted as the leading role in a remade version of Hitchcock's famous movie *Rear Window*. He was able to "write" an autobiography through dictation, aptly called *Still Me*, which was on the *New York Times* bestseller list for eleven straight weeks. In fact, Reeve reached such an extraordinary height, that at one point near the end of his life he said, "I feel happier now than I have ever been in my life."

Perhaps an even more inspiring story is that of Nick Vujicic. Nick was born to an Australian preacher, and sadly born with a rare condition called tetra-amelia syndrome, which meant he had no arms or legs. All that he had were two toes of one foot. His upbringing was one of immense sadness and loneliness, as well as the torments from classmates, stares from strangers everywhere he went, not to mention the enormous difficulties in mobility and function. Nick needed help with everything, from getting dressed, to showering, to eating. And yet, something happened within Nick, as life seemed to get increasingly difficult, his spirit seemed to grow increasingly stronger. He began to look at the challenges that were given to him as a growing opportunity for himself. He learned to type, shave, answer the phone, and much more. He graduated from college at only twenty-one years old in a double-major of accountancy and financial planning. He began to use his own disabilities as a way to help others as well. He started a non-profit called Life without Limbs, and currently lectures all over the world, inspiring people, talking about faith, God, and the incredible potential every human being has, no matter what disabilities they may have. All done by someone with extreme disabilities and yet has risen to heights far greater than people born with no disabilities.

God Carries Us on His Shoulders

One final point about suffering; it is ultimately God who carries us through our difficult times. It is worth repeating the well-known poem about suffering:

> *One night I dreamed I was walking*
> *Along the beach with the Lord,*
> *Many scenes from my life flashed across the sky.*
> *In each scene I noticed footprints in the sand.*
> *Sometimes there were two sets of footprints.*
> *Other times there was only one.*
> *This bothered me because I noticed*
> *During the low periods of my life when I was*
> *Suffering from anguish, sorrow or defeat,*
> *I could see only one set of footprints.*
> *So I said to the Lord, "You promised me,*
> *Lord, that if I followed you,*
> *You would walk with me always.*
> *But I noticed during the most trying periods*
> *Of my life there has only been*
> *One set of prints in the sand.*
> *Why, when I needed you most,*
> *Have you not been there for me?"*
> *The Lord replied,*
> *"The times when you saw only one set of footprints*
> *It was then that I carried you."*

Knowing this can make all the difference in the world. Why God puts us through such difficulties we will never understand, but we can also take comfort in the knowledge that ultimately it is He who carries us through it. It reminds me of one of the most beautiful ideas I have ever read, a comment from the great Alexander Rebbe. He commented on the famous verse from the book of Psalms, "To declare of Your Loving kindness in the morning and of Your Faithfulness in the night." This verse speaks about our love for God's kindness when it is morning, meaning when things are going well for us in our lives, and things are clear to us like daylight. The verse also speaks about having faith even during difficult times, when it is night and the world around seems very dark and frightening. However, the question is, shouldn't the words say in *"our* faithfulness?" For isn't it our faith in God that helps us get through difficult times? The Alexander Rebbe explains beautifully; no it isn't *our* faith that gets us through those times, it is *God's Faith in us* which helps us through difficult times. It is God's Belief in us, and His help which helps us through these times. Knowing this, it is no wonder why so many people can receive so much inspiration and growth during difficult times. It is those times of stormy seas when God is closest to us; He is transporting us on His shoulders to safe land again.

My blessing to all of us is that no one should ever know of suffering. No one should ever be tested in that way. We should only know good news in all of our days. However, if any of us is faced with that challenge, we are able to find the strength to see it as a springboard for spiritual growth and remember God is with us during those moments and He is carrying us through those times.

Spiritual Exercises

1. Try to remember a time of pain and suffering. How did you feel toward God during those times?

2. After a difficult time, how did you feel toward God afterward? Did you feel closer to Him or further away?

3. Think of someone you know who is going through a difficult experience. Have you seen spiritual growth from the person?

4. Think of a famous personality who went through a painful experience, and yet emerged spiritually energized. How do you feel they found the strength to reach greater spiritual heights?

5. Try to think of ways you can emulate this person when you go through a difficult time. In life, we all need role models to coach us through our own travails.

Chapter 5
The Fulfillment of Jewish Outreach

Hillel used to say:
Be among the disciples of Aaron,
Loving peace and pursuing peace,
Loving people and bringing them closer to the Torah.

~ Ethics of the Fathers

I HEARD A HUMOROUS STORY from Rabbi Mark Wildes which has a really beautiful message. The story is about "Dave," a recent *ba'al teshuvah* (returnee to Judaism) who was just starting to learn about Jewish customs and traditions. He wanted desperately to contribute to the new religious community that he was now a part of. He especially wanted to participate in the prayer service, but since Dave didn't know Hebrew, he was limited in what he could do. The *gabbai* (prayer-service coordinator) decided one day that Dave would be able to do *gelilah*, the wrapping the Torah Scroll and putting on the velvet covering. Dave was excited about being given this opportunity and practiced during the week so that he would be able to perform *gelilah* on the Sabbath when the Torah Scroll is taken out and read.

The moment for *gelilah* came and Dave was called up to the area where the Torah was. Dave proudly wrapped the Torah Scroll, fastened it together, and put on the velvet cover. Thinking he was done, he turned to leave, when suddenly the *gabbai* handed him an ornate silver crown. Dave had never seen this part and didn't know what to do with it. He looked back at the *gabbai* with a puzzled looked on his face. The *gabbai* whispered to him "Dave, put it on!" Dave didn't realize that the *gabbai* meant that he should put the silver crown on the top of the Torah Scroll, and mistakenly thought that the *gabbai* meant he should put the crown on himself! So carefully placed the crown on his head, folded his arms, and smiled.

Shortly after this incident took place, the Rabbi of that synagogue was giving a discourse on the teachings of the Maimonides. He came to the section which says, "There are three crowns which have been given to the Jewish People. They are the crown of *Malchut* (Kingship), the crown of *Kehunah* (Priesthood) and the crown of Torah. The crown of Kingship was only given to the descendants of King David; the crown of Priesthood was only given to the descendants of Aaron, but the crown of Torah anyone who wants to can come and put it on.

The Rabbi smiled at this point and said, "Last week many of us may have chuckled at what happened to Dave but in reality he taught us a great lesson. The crown of Torah *is* for anyone. Anyone who wants to can come and put it on."

This is the special uniqueness of Torah. There is something in Torah for everyone. No other study is so rich and multifaceted that it can appeal to virtually everyone. There are parts of Torah that can appeal to the intellectual mind, the rational mind, the mathematical mind, the scientific mind, the medical mind, the mystical mind, the emotional mind, the spiritual mind, or the poetic mind.

This is what reaching out to other Jews is all about; teaching others about how all encompassing Torah is, and how there is something in it for everyone.

Our Actions Make a Difference

I want to share two personal stories. The first occurred during when I was in undergraduate school. At the time I was very confused myself in my Judaism, and really didn't care much for Judaism at all. I enjoyed the freedoms the college life had to offer, and was more than willing to throw off what I perceived to be the shackles of Jewish tradition and dogma. I kept the bare minimum to make my parents happy, and not much more. One day, I was approached by a local Jewish outreach organization which focused on the college campus scene. The representative asked if I could begin studying one-on-one for an hour once a week with an individual from a very limited Jewish background. I saw this is a way to feel I did my one "good deed" for the week so I can enjoy the partying during the rest of the week. And so my studying with Brian, as I shall call him, began. The two of us became good friends, and indeed, he grew a lot from the experience. He went on to go to Israel to study in Ohr Sameach, a religious *yeshivah* for Jews from assimilated backgrounds, and went on to become an observant Jew. But perhaps the most extraordinary aspect to the story is what studying with him did to me. As I was helping Judaism come alive for him, it was coming back to life for me as well. As he grew excited studying the beautiful stories of our Patriarchs and Matriarchs, I found myself growing excited with him, as if I was learning it for the first time as well. I found myself beginning to study Torah more often, but this time with a fresh perspective. And so I was climbing back into Judaism, not out of rote, but out of love. The spark had been ignited in him, but had spread to ignite my own spark as well.

The second story is perhaps even more amazing. This story occurred to me when I was living in Washington Heights in New York City. I was walking to synagogue on Friday just before the Sabbath when I was approached by a young man coming out of the subway. He was dressed a little like a punk, in black leather boots and jacket, and was maybe in his early 20's. He had a slight Russian accent, and told me he is Jewish and had never been inside of a real synagogue before, and was curious to see a prayer service. Since I was on my way anyways, I told him to come with me. He told me he comes from a Russian and assimilated background, and had moved to San Francisco. He said he was visiting New York City for one week, and since he knew so many Jews lived in here, he could get his first Jewish experience. At the time he seemed more curious than anything, not out a desire to learn more about his faith. As fate would have it, that particular night, the prayer service was nicer than usual, with a lot of spirited Carlebach tunes. He followed along in the English, totally transfixed on what was taking place. I explained to him a lot of the meaning and depth behind the Friday night service, and he drank it all in thirstily.

After prayers were over, I asked him if he wanted to join me for the meal. He didn't have any other plans, so he joined me. As fate would have it, I went to a very special family that night, a young couple with an adorable little baby, who helped make it a beautiful warm Sabbath atmosphere. We had a lot of singing, laughter, words of Torah, delicious food, and some friendly chatter as well. I remember the night well, sitting in the soft glow of the Sabbath candles, him drinking in every song and every word about our faith.

By the end of the night, he seemed transformed. He smiled from ear to ear, and said to me, "You know, Yisroel, this is my first Sabbath, and really my first Jewish experience I have ever had. Thank you so much for making it such a beautiful and meaningful one." He took out his pen and paper and asked me for my email address. I explained to him gently that on the Sabbath we don't write, but he can try to remember my email by heart, and gave it to him. He left the meal, looking like a new person.

Sure enough, a few days later, I received an email from him, once again thanking me for the beautiful Sabbath experience. I responded that it was wonderful meeting him, I was so glad he had such an enjoyable experience, and asked him to keep in touch.

I thought' this would be the end of the story. Except for an email I received from him months later, just before the holiday of Rosh Hashanah. The email moved me to tears. He wrote to me that he was now wrapping *tefillin* (phylacteries) on his arm each morning, is keeping the Sabbath every week, and is soon going to Israel to study in *yeshivah*. Life had changed for him dramatically since he discovered the beautiful gift that is Judaism.

This incident, needless to say, made a huge impact on me. It showed me what seemingly small gestures, giving people a little taste of Judaism can indeed transform a person's life forever.

Chabad's Approach

The path of reaching out to other Jews exploded during the birth of Chassidut. The legendary Baal Shem Tov, the founder of the Chassidic movement sought to make Torah not only accessible to the scholars who had the benefit of a rich Torah education, but also to the common folk, the carpenters, the water carriers, the tailors, etc.

YISROEL JUSKOWITZ

The Lubavitcher Rebbe said, "Rabbi Shalom Dobver, of saintly memory, once taught that a 'Chassid is like a street lamp lighter.' In olden days, there was a person in every town who would light the street lamps with a light he carried at the end of a long pole. On the street-corners, the lamps were there in readiness, waiting to be lit; sometimes, however, the lamps are not easily accessible. There are lamps in forsaken places… and there must be someone to light even those lamps, so they may fulfill their purpose and light up the path of others. It is written, 'The soul of man is the candle of God.' It is also written, 'A mitzvah is a candle, and the Torah is light.' A Chassid is one who puts aside his personal affairs and sets out to light up the souls of Jews with the light of Torah and mitzvot. Jewish souls are ready and waiting to be kindled."

However, here the Rebbe added, "This function is not really limited to Chassidim, but is the function of every Jew. Divine Providence brings Jews to the most unexpected, remote places, so that they may carry out this purpose of lighting up the world."

In a very real way, we are all teachers. We make an impact on everyone in everything we do, and everyone we interact with throughout the day. Outreach does not just mean making someone into a practicing observant Jew, as some people think. We are all growing; we all have ways we can grow more. Outreach means to help each other in small ways, whether helping someone from an observant background who is confused about their Judaism, or reaching out to someone with a limited Jewish background. Even studying with someone at the same level is outreach, for you are helping them with their own Torah knowledge. Teaching Torah to others is not limited to only for observant Jews to teach non-observant Jews, or Jews who have not had the privilege of receiving a Jewish education.

It is fulfilling to teach everyone, whether observant or not. When one realizes he or she has something precious, it is only natural to want to share it with everyone.

Someone once asked the Rebbe why the mission of the Lubavitch Chassid is to put on *tefillin* in the street, or hand out Shabbat candles to men and women whom they have met before. The Rebbe, in his inimitable fashion answered, "Because of what they already *are,* not because of not because of what they may *become.*" Not so that he or she may one day become "Orthodox," but because right now they are already Jewish, and *tefillin* and Shabbat candles *belong* to them; it is their right and their obligation to perform the mitzvah, and it is our privilege, honor, and obligation to respectfully help them do so, with the same fervor and compassion that I would provide a warm meal and a place to sleep for a passerby whom I have never seen before and may never see again.

This can be seen from the verse in the Torah, "The Torah was commanded to Moses, it is an inheritance for all of the assembly of Jacob." This means that Torah is not only limited to the scholars or the fully observant Jews, but it is an inheritance to *all* of Israel.

Rewards for Teaching Others

It is important to note that the role of teacher applies to all of us, regardless of our level of observance or not. For ultimately we all have our own unique strengths in our knowledge and service of God. We are all still learning and growing. And we can all be teachers. The rewards for helping a fellow Jew discover his or her Torah heritage is eternal. The Talmud writes that whoever teaches his fellow Torah is regarded by Scripture as if he 'made' that person. This is as the verse writes regarding our holy father Abraham, who taught Judaism to the people of the city of Haran, "And the souls that they *made* in Haran." Furthermore, the Talmud records another opinion that says Scripture regards him as if he "made" the words of the Torah. This is indicated from the verse, "If you preserve the words of this covenant, you will make them," referring to the Torah as a covenant. The commentaries explain that this verse teaches that *if you preserve the words of this covenant* in your mouth, to impart them to your fellow, then *you will make them.* This means you will create new words of Torah, new perceptions and insights that you have brought into the world as a result of your teaching. This is in conjunction with the teaching from the Sages that while a person learns much from his teachers and even more from his colleagues, he learns the most from his students.

However, perhaps the greatest of the opinions in the Talmud on this subject is that if one teaches his fellow Torah, Scripture regards him as if he made *himself.* This is derived from the same verse just quoted "you will make them." This last word *otam*, "them," can also be read *attem*, "you." Thus the verse reads, "you will make *you.*" This is an incredible lesson about the power of teaching someone else words of Torah; it has the power to create *you*, meaning you will not be the same person after teaching them. Rather, you will be one step higher, one step closer to the divine image inside of us.

From all of the years that I have been involved in outreach, I have seen numerous times how much this is true. Sometimes, after teaching an idea, concept, or law within Judaism, it awakens something powerful inside of me that would have otherwise lain dormant. This is inherent energy within the Torah, the ability to create a greater self-awareness just from imparting Torah to others.

And how great is the reward for causing one's fellow man to perform a mitzvah? The Talmud writes that Scripture regards him as if he performed the mitzvah himself. This is derived from the verse regarding Moses' staff, which began the first of the Ten Plagues in Egypt, "And your staff with which you struck the river." However, the Torah tells us that it was Aaron who started the first of the Ten Plagues! (Moses did not want to strike the Nile River to turn the water into blood since the river had saved him when he was put in a basket and sent afloat from the pursuing Egyptians.) So why does Scripture state that Moses struck it? This is to teach us this great lesson; for by Moses passing on the staff to Aaron to give him the privilege of obeying God's word, Scripture regards Moses as if he performed it himself.

Our great forefather Abraham, the world's first Jew, spent much of his life reaching out to the pagan world around him, teaching everyone he encountered about monotheism, morality, and kindness. The Talmud teaches that the actions of our forefathers are a sign for how we, as his children should lead our lives. Thus this trait of imparting the beauty of Judaism to others was instilled in us since the very inception of our faith nearly four thousand years ago.

Teaching Through Action

Teaching about Judaism can be through action as well. When one acts in a way that reflects the values of our People, it inspires those around him or her to appreciate what Judaism can be. One of the famous stories told over about Rabbi Shlomo Carlebach was when he was once giving a concert in Haight-Ashbury, a neighborhood in San Francisco. In the back sat someone noticeably deformed. Everyone who was nearby shuttered to look at him and so naturally he sat all alone. In the middle of the concert, Rabbi Carlebach noticed the man and ran over to him. "You are so beautiful, my friend!" he exclaimed and hugged the man. Stunned, the man, who obviously longed for an embrace, hugged Shlomo back. The two sat there for awhile, when tears started to trickle down the man's cheeks. Suddenly, the audience burst into song. One person in the audience, a secular and assimilated Jew was so moved by this incredible act of compassion that he started thinking about how special Judaism must be and the heights that a sincerely religious person can reach. Just from witnessing this one act, this person set off to explore his heritage in Israel, and today is a respected observant rabbi who teaches advanced Talmud classes.

The heights that one can reach who became observant on their own are perhaps even higher than those who have been observant all of their lives. The Talmud writes, "In a place where *ba'alei teshuvah* stand, even the righteous do not stand." This is because they are people who came from almost nothing, and embraced Judaism with passion and a sense of newness. They took that faithful, courageous and often difficult leap, sometimes against the wishes of those who are important to them in their lives, into traditional observant Judaism. This is a feat which is unparalleled to anything anyone who was born observant can ever do. This is why often *ba'alei teshuvah* surpass their Jewish counterparts who were already born observant.

The Greatest Returnee: Rabbi Akiva

In the Talmud we are told of the greatest returnee to Judaism of all time, the great Sage Rabbi Akiva. Rabbi Akiva was ignorant for much of his life; he was a Shepherd, which was considered at the time to be an occupation for the lower class. Moreover, Rabbi Akiva despised Torah scholars, declaring that if he saw a scholar he would want to run over to him and bite him like a donkey.

And then something Rabbi Akiva once saw changed his life forever. It was nothing so awe-inspiring or incredible, just a simple wondrous occurrence in nature. He once passed by a stream and saw water dripping onto a rock. Over a great deal of time, the water bore a small hole through the rock. This made an indelible impression on him. Rabbi Akiva said to himself, "If water can eventually penetrate through rock, perhaps the Torah, which is compared to water, can penetrate the rock which is my heart."

So at the age of forty, Rabbi Akiva began to study Hebrew, even though it meant studying together with little children who were also learning the *aleph-bet*. His thirst for knowledge grew more, and so he decided to go to *yeshivah*, with the support and blessing of his wife. He spent seven years studying, and upon returning home, he overheard his some of his neighbors ridiculing his wife that her husband has all but completely abandoned her. His wife exclaimed, "If it was up to me, I would want my husband to be away for another seven years!" When hearing this, Rabbi Akiva returned to *yeshivah* and studied for another seven years.

When Rabbi Akiva emerged, he was no longer the simple shepherd, but a powerful Sage who had over 24,000 students. So great was Rabbi Akiva's Torah knowledge, that the Midrash writes he was able to even expound on the crowns on the tops of the letters in the Torah scroll and gain deeper meaning and understanding, a feat which even our great teacher Moses was unable to do. Rabbi Akiva became famous for preaching that the Torah's commandment "You shall love your neighbor as yourself" is *the* most fundamental principal in the entire Torah. Furthermore, Rabbi Akiva taught the importance of honoring Torah scholars; one should honor them nearly as much as one honor's God, for they are the messenger's of His Word. Hard to believe that this is the same Rabbi Akiva who once said he would run over to any Torah scholar and bite him like a donkey!

The Talmud records an unbelievable story about what occurred at the end of Rabbi Akiva's life. Torah study was forbidden by the Romans, with the penalty of death for one who transgresses the decree. Nevertheless, Rabbi Akiva continued to study and to teach. When someone asked him if he is afraid of the Romans, he replied with the following parable:

"A fox saw some fish swimming rapidly. 'What are you swimming away from?' he asked the fish. 'From the fisherman's net,' they replied. The fox asked slyly, 'Why don't you come up onto dry land over here where it will be safe? There aren't any fisherman's nets here!' The fish replied, 'You are supposed to be the wisest of all animals? You are a fool! If here in the water, which is the environment we need to be in to live, yet still we are afraid, how much more afraid we will be if we were to be on dry land!"

"So it is with Torah," Rabbi Akiva said. "Torah is the life force that sustains us, as the verse write, 'For it is your life, and it will lengthen your days.' If without Torah, we cannot *live*, how much more frightening the world would be without it!"

Sadly enough, Rabbi Akiva eventually was caught and brought before the Romans in their coliseum for execution. They began combing his flesh with iron combs, when Rabbi Akiva realized it was time to say the *Shema*, the special prayer which declares the sovereignty of God. At this point Rabbi Akiva's students cried out, "Teacher, even now? Even now you recite the *Shema*?" Rabbi Akiva responded, "Yes, even now. For it says in the *Shema* to love God with all of your soul, which I always interpreted to mean even if one has to give up one's soul. All of these years I wondered if I would ever be able to have the opportunity to fulfill this precept, and now that it is in my hand, should I not fulfill it?" As Rabbi Akiva finished the word *echad* ("one"), declaring the Oneness of God, a Heavenly voice then rang out, "Great is the sage Rabbi Akiva, for he will sit in the Garden of Eden for all eternity!"

This is the height that one can reach with *teshuvah*. Rabbi Akiva came from nothing, ran to Judaism and embraced it, reaching to a sublime level unattainable by nearly anyone who ever lived.

Seeking the Spark

One of my favorite Chabad stories is about two *sheluchim* (Chabad messengers) who were in Jacksonville, Florida. They pulled in to a gas station to fill up on gas, and a giant person who looked like a thug told them there is someone in the back of the store wanted to speak to them. Frightened, the two of them made their way to the back of the store and saw an old man sitting there. The old man started speaking to them in Yiddish. He told them that he came from a Chassidic family and was a Holocaust survivor. His wife and children were killed in the war, and he moved to America to a Chassidic community in Williamsburg. When he got to Williamsburg, he saw Jews living comfortably eating delicious foods. He felt disgusted that Jews were living so comfortably in America while their brethren had been going through Hell in Europe. Frustrated, he left Judaism altogether, married someone who was not Jewish, had children together and moved to Florida, never telling any of them that he was Jewish.

Many years went by, and he had already turned eighty years old. One night in his home, he couldn't sleep, so he went downstairs and turned on the television. On the news was about a big gathering of Jews in Brooklyn, and the late Lubavitcher Rebbe was speaking. He was speaking in Yiddish, his mother language, and the translation was on the bottom of the screen. The segment that was on the news was the Rebbe was saying the following words, "It is written in Isaiah, 'And God is going to gather one by one the Jewish People.' Rashi says each Jew is going to be grabbed by the collar and brought back to Jerusalem. This to mean every Jew no matter where they are and how removed they are from Judaism; every Jew has a giant soul with a piece of Godliness who stood on Mount Sinai. And there will be a day *that you cannot sleep*, because you know that one day you will be taken and brought back home."

He revealed himself that night to his family that he was Jewish and his first family had been killed in Auschwitz and one day he will be taken back home to his people. And sure enough, only a couple of days later these two Chabad messengers pulled up to his gas station! He told his son he wanted to speak to them. The story goes on to say that they helped him put up *mezuzot* in the doorway and helped make the kitchen kosher. Afterwards he called up one of the messengers and thanked him for helping try to be the Jew that he knew he could be and secretly longed to be. A couple of weeks after the phone call, he passed away.

The lesson of the story is very powerful. Jews are everywhere, hidden Jews, Jews who had left their heritage years ago, but still deep down may yearn for their faith, and can be inspired no matter where they are, no matter what age they may be.

Let us all learn from these great lessons, return to God wholeheartedly and inspire others to return as well.

Spiritual Exercises

1. Try to think of a time in your life when you helped someone else discover Judaism. How did you feel at the time? How did you feel afterwards?

2. Try to think of a time when you taught someone Torah or about Jewish beliefs. How did you feel at the time? How did you feel afterwards?

3. Try to think of someone you know who is very confused about their Judaism or has a very limited Jewish background. Try to think of ways you can help them fulfill their Jewish destiny or teach that person more about their faith. Then monitor how this involvement changes your day and your life.

4. Try to think of a Jewish outreach organization that you feel connected to and appreciate their work. Try to think of some ways you can get involved with the organization, and contributing in any small way you can. Then monitor how this involvement changes your day and your life.

Chapter 6
Connecting Through Creativity

The power of imagination makes us infinite.

~ John Muir

CREATIVITY IS POWER. I LOVE the quote above, because it sums up the awesome potential inherent in expressing creativity. This was a gift bestowed upon Man and Man alone. Every other living creature lives only to survive, whereas Man can live to create. Only Man can create music, beautiful works, of art, skyscrapers, sculptures, books, poetry, and of course novel ideas in Torah. One of the running themes throughout this book is the idea of partnering with God, or mimicking His ways as a way to get closer to Him. In fact, it was, as discussed previously a Biblical commandment, "You shall walk in His ways." This has many ramifications, as discussed in the chapter of Love and the chapter on Kindness. However, I believe in this chapter, it has the greatest ramification of all. For I know, and have experienced firsthand, the great lengths that people will go to (including myself) to express their own creativity. I have seen "starving artists," with families, who spend every moment they can, often giving up easier and better ways to earn a living so they can pursue their own creative endeavors. An old friend of mine in high school once turned down a scholarship in Princeton in the field of Neuroscience so he could become a full-time artist since he felt it would give him a greater sense of fulfillment. Where does this drive come from? Why would a human being possibly push off some of the basic needs of survival to pursue their creative potential? Does it come from a Divine source? Can it be channeled as a way to get closer to Him? Does it have destructive potential as well?

The Power of Music

Let us discuss first one of the greatest and most common forms of creativity; namely music, for in music lies many of the answers to these questions.

Music is perhaps one of the greatest forces that God has given to Man and it remains up to Man how to utilize this creative energy. Music can be far more than mere entertainment or something to help us relax. Music is very much like fire. Like fire, music can destroy. Sadly enough in our generation many people have committed terrible destructive acts and said they were inspired by music to do them.

However, also like fire, music has the ability to provide warmth, to heal, and to create positive energy. Also in our generation, we have seen the incredible power of Rabbi Shlomo Carlebach's immortal melodies that inspired thousands to become *ba'alei teshuvah*. Music has the power to speak in a way which words can never do, and can reach far deeper places. Rabbi Shneur Zalman of Liadi once said, "Words are the pen of the heart, but music is the pen of the soul." Indeed Reb Shlomo's music taught me the power of the melody, and inspired me to unlock the music contained within my own soul. Music has the ability to transform the person. It is interesting to note, the *Shelah HaKodesh* points out that the Hebrew word for music is *zemer,* which contains the same root letters of *zamor,* "prune, cut off the bad parts of a plant." What connection is there between music and pruning? He explains that music has the ability to *prune one's character,* to refine the person's soul and make him or her into a better person.

Where do we see in the Torah the power of the melody? Rabbi Moshe Weinberger said a great teaching from Rabbi Nachman of Breslov about the power of music. A *metzora* (a leper) must atone for his sin of speaking *lashon hara*, (slander, gossip) about his fellow man by bringing to birds that are pure as a sacrifice. What connection is there between speaking badly about one's fellow man and bringing a sacrifice of two birds? The answer is that this man uttered a sound from his lips that was impure when he spoke badly about another person. Therefore, the only rectification can be through an utterance, or *sound* of purity. Birds, as we all know are famous for their ability to sing. Furthermore, it is specifically through a bird that is *pure,* meaning in the spiritual sense unscathed by the physical world. This is the power of music; the ability to transform that which is impure into something pure.

Rebbe Nachman further writes that many of the prophets would first have music played to them to put them into the proper mood for prophesy. King David was famous for playing the harp before writing the Psalms. Indeed, David would begin many of his Psalms with the word song, as in the famous Psalm "A Song of Ascents." The Talmud tells us that David would arise early in the morning to study Torah and pray after the east wind would wake him by blowing through a wind chime, creating music.

Rabbi Nachman also writes that this is why the Hebrew word for a cantor is a "Chazzan." This comes from the same root as *chazon*, "vision." This is because someone who leads the congregation in song and prayer with a sincere heart is connecting to God in a very similar way to prophecy.

The very first song we encounter in the Torah is the song the Jewish People sang after the sea split, destroying the Egyptian army, thereby bringing them salvation. The Midrash writes that the level of closeness to God was so great at that moment that even a simple maidservant was capable of achieving a higher degree of revelation greater than Ezekiel did in the famous Vision he had at the beginning of the Book of Ezekiel. The *Midrash* further writes that it was only at this moment that they were able to sing because they were able to see how all the different facets of Creation and History fit together like one beautiful harmony. The Zohar writes that the Jewish People did not want to leave the sea because of what they had witnesses and the ecstasy they experienced until God compelled them to leave.

The Torah writes out the beautiful and poetic words to the song, which was led by our Teacher Moses with his sister Miriam the Prophetess and the other women accompanying with drums. If one looks at the text, one sees that there are many spaces between the words. What is the reason for this? We find a similar phenomenon much later in the Torah when Moses sings a final farewell song to the Jewish People. The reason for this, Rabbi Aron Soloveichik writes, is to teach us that there is the real song, which is beyond the words, which can never be put into words, which represents the pure melody as well as to convey the depth and the emotion experienced at that time.

Even the Torah is referred to as a song, as it says near the end of Deuteronomy, "And now it is time to write down this song." This is because of the intense emotional experience that one can achieve when studying Torah, one can begin to think of the Torah as one long beautiful melody. It is perhaps for this reason that the final words that Moses said to the Jewish people in the Torah were expressed as a song. Furthermore, song is one of the ways we can serve God. In the times of the First and Second Temple, the Levites would sing praises to God while standing on the fifteen steps leading to the inside of the Temple. The Levites' part of the service was almost as much of an integral part of the service as the Priests' service in the Temple.

Nowadays, when there is no Temple, we still retain the tradition of song in our daily prayers. On the Sabbath and on all of the Jewish Holidays we use song as part of our services to enhance the meaning of the words. In the daily prayers, we say the verse from Chronicles, "Sing to Him, make music to Him, speak of all His wonders." On Yom Kippur, the holiest day of the Jewish calendar, we say in the liturgy, "I shall put my hope in God, I shall beseech his presence, I shall request of Him eloquent speech. So that I can sing of His strength in the people's congregation, that I can express glad songs for the sake of His human creations." Once again, we see the important role that song plays in glorifying God's Great Name. One of the most beautiful poems in the entire prayer book is the *Anim Zemirot*, "Song of Glory," written by the great twelfth-century Kabbalist Rabbi Yehudah He-Chassid. This song is considered so sublime, that the ark is opened and many congregations consider us unworthy to sing this song every Sabbath and reserve it only for the High Holy Days. The opening words to this poem are "I shall compose pleasant psalms and weave beautiful hymns because for You my soul shall pine."

Another power that music has is the ability to lift up someone's spirits no matter where that person is, or whatever state they are in. Many of us have had this out of body experience when hearing and feeling a beautiful melody. There is a story told by Yaffa Eliach about a fourteen-year-old boy named Moshe who was brought to Mauthausen concentration camp in 1944. The boy was a pupil of the great Bobover Rebbe.

The story took place during one of the awful roundups that the Nazis used to enforce each morning in the camps. If someone was missing, all of the inmates were forced to wait, standing naked in the freezing cold until everyone was accounted for. On this particular bitter cold winter day, one person was missing. The hours began to pass as the people were forced to stand in the cold. One by one, people began freezing to death and dropping onto the snow covered ground.

Young Moshe also felt himself beginning to freeze, as his limbs began to turn numb. Suddenly he heard the great Bobover Rebbe in his mind telling him to sing, telling him a Chassid must always sing. He closed his eyes, absorbed himself completely in the soulful melodies of Bobov, and impossibly even began to dance. He was so completely enraptured in the melody till it filled his body and soul, and barely even realized the roundup was over. His heart felt warm from the fire of the Bobov melody. The melody that morning saved his life.

Thus we see the sublime heights that one can reach through music. One's body can be in the depths of hell and his spirit can sour completely above the shackles of his physical body. Natan Sharansky, the famous Soviet Refusnik once said that the Carlebach songs *Am Yisrael Chai!* ("The Jewish People Live!) and *Yisrael Betach Bashem* ("The Jewish People Have Faith in God") gave him tremendous strength as he sat in a cold hard Russian prison. He also said that the song with the immortal words of Rabbi Nachman of Breslov, "The world is a very narrow bridge. In order to cross it, one must be without fear," gave him hope and joy in the darkest of days.

Jewish music has the ability to not only tell the story of the Jewish People, but to capture the mood of the story. When one sings *Nachamu Ami* ("Be Comforted, My People") melody, one can really become a part of Jewish history and feel as if they were standing in Jerusalem next to the great prophet Isaiah hearing him comfort his People on the loss of the Holy Temple. When one hears *Veshavu Banim* ("My Children Will Return"), one can hear the great prophets singing, instilling hope to the People that the Great Day will come soon. When one hears *Al Eileh Ani Bochia* ("On This I Am Crying") one can hear the prophet Jeremiah weeping over the destruction of Jerusalem.

The Power of Art

It is important to remember that music is only one of the great channels that God has given to Man to express his creativity. There are so other avenues, and these too can bring closeness to God. We see throughout the ages the use of creative writing as a way to enhance one's spirituality; from Kings David and Solomon, through the prayers and songs of the Kabbalists, and the imaginative poetry of Rabbi Abraham Isaac Kook.

One of the other ways to express creativity is through art. We see from the Torah that God endowed people with the gift of creativity and artistic expression and it is gift that can be used to deepen our connection to God. In the Book of Exodus, God designated the task of designing the Tabernacle that would accompany the Jewish People in the wilderness to a thirteen-year-old boy named Betzalel. The verse writes, "See, God has proclaimed by name, Betzalel, son of Uri son of Hur, of the tribe of Judah. He filled him with Godly spirit, with wisdom, insight, and knowledge, and with every craft—to weave designs, to work with gold, silver, and copper, stone-cutting for setting, and wood-carving—to perform every craft of design." From here we see that art is a talent given directly from God and it was intended as a way of beautifying our service to God. In fact, the Talmud writes that the name "Betzalel" actually comes from the words *betzel El*, which mean, "in the shadow of God." This means that Betzalel was, so to speak, in God's Shadow, for he was doing God's holy work and was an extension of his hand. Rabbi Abraham Isaac Kook helped begin the Betzalel School of Art in Israel, designed to promote art in the context of Judaism and spirituality.

In Chapter 1, we mentioned the Talmudic passage based on the verse "There is no Rock [*Tzur*] like our God" which the Talmud expounds exegetically to read, "There is no Artist [*Tziar*] like our God." This exposition has very deep ramifications. For by creating beautiful works of art, we are, in a very real way, emulating God's way, who is the Ultimate Artist.

We also see the concept of beautifying our service to God through art from the first Holy Temple built by King Solomon. The Talmud writes that if someone who did not see the Temple in the days of Solomon, that person has never witnessed true beauty. The Talmud writes that the walls of the Temple were made of different colored exotic stones of blue and green and gave the illusion of the waves of the ocean. Furthermore, much of the Temple was made of solid gold and silver. King Solomon went to painstaking extremes to make the Temple exquisitely beautiful to glorify God's Name in His dwelling place here on earth. There were handcrafted angels on the top of the ark, their wings stretching and touching one another. There were flowers and buttercups engraved into the Temple Menorah.

As a practicing Judaic artist for many years, I have been privileged to feel an attachment to God when I draw and paint. Often I can feel God's comforting Hand, so to speak, resting on my hand guiding me through the motions and helping me to create works of art. When I draw the portraits of our spiritual leaders, I can feel the presence of the great sage speaking to me, and comforting me. When I draw the great symbols of the Sabbath I can feel the great tranquility of the Sabbath descending upon me even though it is in the middle of the week. When I create a piece of art with the Prayer for the Welfare of the State of Israel, I can picture a holy soldier standing next to me with a rifle in his hand, protecting our sacred land from dangerous enemies. When I draw a piece on the imminent Redemption, it transports me into a different world and I long for that Great Day. This is what creativity can do for a person; a deep expression of one's innermost soul.

Much like music, visual art has the ability to not only tell the story of our People, but to capture the mood of the story as well. When one sees a beautiful painting of the great Biblical scenes drawn by a prolific artist, we can almost feel as if we are there, capturing the moment of the splitting of the sea, of the triumphant moment when Jacob defeated the angel of Esau, or see Jacob's dream of a ladder going up into eternity with angels ascending to Heaven and descending to Earth. One can experience the moment when God halted Abraham at the very last moment as he held the blade over his beloved son Isaac and informed that he was testing Abraham's loyalty, and Abraham will have children as numerous as the stars of the sky. One can feel the moment when Joseph, the viceroy in Egypt, revealed himself to his brothers, showing the fulfillment of his dreams. In modern day history, too, paintings on the Holocaust reflect the saddest chapter in our history and paintings on the birth of the State of Israel help us remember our most glorious ones.

One really great privilege that one has as a Judaic artist is painting the majestic landscapes and holy sites of the Land of Israel. Artwork can capture its true beauty much more than mere photographs. Rabbi Kook, who was well versed in art history and many art techniques, once told artist the Herman Shtruck, who lived in the Land of Israel, "You are an emissary duty-bound to reveal the beauty and sanctity of our holy land, to sketch historic localities, the sight of which will awaken affection for the Land and stir yearnings for its mountains and valleys." He concluded with a blessing, "May the Holy One, who placed in the heart of Betzalel and Ohaliav the wisdom to build the Tabernacle, continue to grant wisdom of the heart to all those who devote their craftsmanship to the Jewish People and the Land of Israel."

Furthermore, we become partners with God when we are involved in creation, as God made this world incomplete and it is up to man to complete it. The Talmud records a fascinating dialogue between a prominent Roman leader and the great sage Rabbi Akiva. The Roman leader asked Rabbi Akiva "What is greater; Man's actions or God's actions?" Surprisingly, Rabbi Akiva answered, "It is Man's actions." He then went ahead and got wheat and cake and asked the Roman officer, "Which of these two is more desirable?" The Roman leader of course answered, "The cake." Rabbi Akiva responded that it is God who makes the wheat, but it is Man who makes the cake." This concept will be revisited later in the chapter on kindness. However, on a simple level this means that God left this world in an incomplete state and by man being involved in creation, he is thereby perfecting the world.

Yisroel Juskowitz

The Power of the Imagination

Rabbi Kook writes extensively about the power of the imagination. Indeed, he writes that the Prophets in the Torah had to use their imaginative faculties to experience God. Scholarship and piety alone was not enough. For in order to experience revelation one must be able to look beyond oneself and into the world that he does not see. God is beyond our understanding and so it takes our powers beyond our reason to experience Him. This is perhaps why the Talmud states that a dream is one-sixtieth prophecy. This is because when one dreams, he or she is cut off from reality. We perceive things differently when we are asleep and suddenly the impossible seems quite possible. The line between what is real and what is surreal becomes blurred. Our reasoning faculties and the imagination takes over. This is perhaps why Samuel and many other prophets were only able to receive prophecy when they were sleeping.

However, a word of caution must be stated. Excessive imagination and passion has its drawbacks, and can be potentially dangerous, even in the realm of spirituality. We see this from the story in the Book of Leviticus in the story of two of Aaron's sons, Nadab and Abihu. Nadab and Abihu were exceptionally pious young men, who served in the Tabernacle with great enthusiasm. They had a tremendous amount of creative energy, and they yearned to get closer to God in a way that even Moses wasn't able to. And so one day they did. They entered the Holy of Holies with an "alien fire before the Lord, which He commanded them not." Moreover, some commentators say they were intoxicated with wine, as they sought to be in a state of ecstasy when entering God's innermost chambers. The verse tells us of their demise; they were consumed fire, "And there went out fire from the Lord and devoured them…." The punishment certainly is measure for measure; they sinned with fire and they were punished by fire. However, perhaps the poetic justice runs even deeper. Fire, as mentioned in the beginning of this chapter has the ability to provide warmth and energy, when *controlled,* when it is a tool in the hands of its master. But fire, when it is not controlled, has only the ability to harm and to destroy. Nadab and Abihu's passion and imagination were powerful and unique, but also it was unbridled. It knew no bounds. The *Midrash* tells us they believed they should add to their love of God a greater and stronger love. A love so strong, that they themselves were consumed in it. The verse is teaching us that our passions must still be guided by Jewish Law for only then is it really desirable by God. Imagination beyond Jewish and doctrine is traveling into forbidden lands, it is an alien fire that God had not commanded.

So it is of utmost importance to use our imagination to create positive beauty in the world and not create things which are detrimental to the spiritual well-being of the world. For ultimately it is up to us what we choose to create. In the words of the great playwright George Bernard Shaw, "Imagination is the beginning of creation. You imagine what you desire, you will what you imagine, and at last, you create what you will."

I hope and pray that each and every one of us uses the hidden creative energies within all of us to glorify God's Great Name, complete and beautify His world, and in the process bring ourselves and others closer to Him.

Spiritual Exercises

1. Try to remember a time when you were express-ing your own creativity. It could be in any area, whether art, music, writing, photography, film, or any other medium. How did you feel at the time? Did you feel any connection to God? Did you feel inspired?

2. Try to think of a creative project you have always wanted to do. Try to take at least a few minutes each day to express your creativity with this proj-ect. Set realistic goals, breaking the project into small increments over time. Then document how you feel while you are working on the project.

3. Try to think of some creative project to bring yourself and others closer to God. If possible, try to begin working on the project. Set realistic goals, and document how you feel when working on the project.

Chapter 7
Prayer:
Transforming Our World, Transforming Ourselves

We do not step out of our world when we pray; we merely see the world in a different setting. The self is not the hub, but the spoke of the revolving wheel. In prayer, we shift the center of living from self-consciousness to self-surrender. God is the center toward which all forces tend. He is the force, and we are the flowing of His force, the ebb and flow of His tides.

~ Abraham Joshua Heschel

IMAGINE YOU ARE INVITED TO a private meeting with the President of the United States. In it, you can tell him all about yourself, and ask for everything that you want and need in life, as well as the needs of your family and community. Tepidly, you walk into the Oval Office, in awe of everything that you see. You know that few people are granted such a privilege. Many would have to pay a great deal of money for such a meeting, but you are given this opportunity for free.

When you go inside, you are escorted to a large comfortable seat by a Secret Service agent, who then leaves, allowing you and the President to be alone. The President looks deeply into your eyes. You know at this moment you have his full undivided attention.

"Mr. President," you begin. Suddenly, instead of slowly articulating your requests, you begin blabbering. "Blah, blah, blah, blah, babababababababababalalalalalala," you rush out your ideas and requests as quickly as possible in a completely incoherent silly fashion, without any emotion, talking faster than an auctioneer in a packed room, and then bolt from the room in a few minutes.

This parable may sound silly, but in reality this is what many of us do when we pray. We all know it is a chance to meet one on one with the Master of the World, sing his praises, and discuss our needs. It is our moment. Many of us have been doing it all of our lives, but of course, therein lies part of the problem. How are we to understand this? Prayer, at best for most of us, is a ritual, a chore, at worst, a nuisance hindering us from doing things we would rather be doing.

We live in an A.D.D. generation. This doesn't mean more people are born with A.D.D., it means more people are producing symptoms of A.D.D. In fact, Adderall, together with anti-depressants, are among the most heavily prescribed medications in the world today. And it is not just in children any more, the frequency in adults now is nearly as high at it is in children. Much of this, I am certain can be attributed to the high-tech, fast paced society that we live in today. We are constantly seeking out stimulation, often with our blackberries, iPhones, iPads, and other electronic devices that can satisfy any momentary boredom and are always ready with a quick distraction. Movies, television, and video games constantly need to be brighter, faster, louder, more graphic and more colorful to maintain our attention. Teachers in the classroom need to be using the latest gadgets to maintain the student's attention, whether it is Power Point, interactive educational tools, computer programs etc. I must admit, I am certainly guilty of this too. I find it difficult sometimes to make it to the end of a YouTube video, even a well-made one! People are constantly texting, during class, during sermons, even during marriage ceremonies. Sadly enough, many people even do the dangerous stunt of texting when driving, as they feel they constantly need to be doing something and driving alone just seems too boring.

What has this done to our generation? Many of us have forgotten what it means to stop and listen, especially to stop and listen to our souls. We have become so caught up in the rat race, so we have often stopped to listen and think about what it all means.

The Sages knew all of this, even thousands of years ago. In fact, one term in Talmud for prayer is *avodah she-ba-lev,* "service of the heart." Another word for prayer is *hitpallel,* which comes from the same root as *po'el,* meaning "work." The Sages were acutely aware that praying indeed takes a great deal of work. This is especially true because of how many times we pray in our daily lives. A short calculation of how many prayers we do, assuming we stick to the prescribed number of three prayers a day as specified according to Jewish Law, is 1,095 prayers in a year! And if an average lifetime is eighty years, a person is praying 87,600 times, and that is not even including the extra prayer service said on the Sabbath and other holidays!

So how can we possibly make our prayers more meaningful? There are certainly no easy answers. But some of the answers may be in relooking at what prayers are supposed to be.

Is prayer only about getting what we want from God? Or is prayer even more about building something within ourselves? And if it is, what is that we are building? In truth, there seems to be so many unanswered questions, when it comes to prayer, almost as many as we have about suffering. Doesn't God already know what we are going to ask for? And doesn't he already know what the outcome will be? And if we don't get the answer we want, don't we have the right to be angry at God for not helping us? And if we don't feel any of what we are saying, but are just reading the words, do we fulfill our obligation to pray?

Once again, as with the subject of suffering, we don't know all of the answers. And the few answers that we do have often don't seem to be as strong as the questions. However, I believe we can circumvent a lot of the questions by at least following an approach. Although this approach may not answer all of the questions, it can provide us with some guidance and this guidance can indeed help make our prayers more meaningful.

Prayer as a Vehicle to Express Our Love

I want to share a story that happened to me awhile ago regarding two people we will call Adam, and his wife, Rebecca. At the time I was still single, and most of my friends were married, and I assumed, happily married. Adam I remembered was so ecstatic at the time of his wedding. When he would talk about his wife, he would talk the way many newlyweds do; his eyes would kind of glaze over and he would talk about all of her wonderful virtues and how he was the luckiest guy in the world to have her. Now flash nine years forward and three kids later. We had been in touch over the years, but most of the time just short phone calls or emails. The two of us had arranged to meet in a café to catch up. Right away, I could tell he was distraught. He seemed edgy and worried, and just generally distracted. His usual gleam in his eyes wasn't there. I asked him what was wrong.

"Well," he started to confide in me and then paused. "Can I share a secret with you? And promise not to judge me?"

"I will try my best," I told him. "And I am here to help."

So he began to confide in me about his marriage problems. How his wife Rebecca asked him to do a lot of the shopping, help put the kids to sleep and help with his kids' homework. Yes, it was true that she often did it a lot too, but he worked longer hours than she did, and he came back from work more exhausted than her. But even bigger than this was just the feeling of mostly being disinterested in her. He didn't have the same feeling of being "in love" with her. He said he didn't hate her, but just didn't have the same strong feelings for her that he once had. He didn't think too much about cheating on her, but he did at times miss the freedom he once had had when he was single. Sometimes he wanted to just get out and see a movie, but she always seemed to want to do some sort of menial chore around the house. Adam told me that he was strongly considering separating for a little while to clear his head, and then see if he still wanted to remain married to her.

"Do you have any advice?" he asked, in an exasperated, defeated tone. His tone suggested he didn't really expect me to say anything insightful, just give him validation to go ahead with his plans. And here he was, going to a single guy to ask for marriage advice! I felt like it was trying to go to John Candy to ask for advice on how to lose weight!

I slowly sipped my coffee and thought deeply about his dilemma. It was hard to believe that my friend, who seemed so fiercely in love with his wife when he got married, now seriously, was considering separating from her. Suddenly an idea occurred to me, and I sat up in my chair.

"I think I have something that may work. Can you write up a list of all the qualities you liked in your wife when you married her? And then I want you to verbally read that list to her. And I don't want you to only do it once. I want you to read it to her three times every day, once in the morning, once in the afternoon, and once at night. And if you can, try to muster up some feeling and think about these qualities about her as you are reading them. I also want your wife to do the same thing for you. I don't want you to just do this for one day, I want you to do this for an entire month. But report back to me in two weeks how it is working for you."

My friend looked at me like I had just landed from some distant planet and was just coming in contact with the human species. "Are you smoking something? Because whatever it is, I might want some of it. Where on earth did you get such a crazy idea from?"

I said, "Well, truthfully, I got the idea from *davening*. If you think about it, most of us go about our day not really feeling a connection to God at all, or even a desire to get close to Him. However, at some point in our lives we all felt a very strong and powerful love for Him, and I believe, His love for us. But we go about our day, and often think of our relationship with God as nothing more than a burden at best. Prayer is the time of the day when we try, as best as we can, to renew our relationship with God. We do this by repeating the qualities we know about Him and the goodness that He has bestowed into the world and into ourselves. And at times we don't feel the words we are saying. But sometimes just saying the words helps us to remember our love for Him. It helps to realign ourselves to what is best for us."

My friend groaned, "Oh Yisroel, you and your spirituality stuff! You should have either been a rabbi or a new age guru... Not sure which one suits you better!"

I smiled, "I am not sure if you meant that as a compliment, but I will take it as one. Either way, will you promise me you will at least try it?"

Reluctantly, he promised me, and we made up to speak again in a couple of weeks. In a couple of weeks he called me up, "Hey Yisroel, guess what," he said wryly. Immediately, I could sense the "I told you so" tone in his voice. "So I tried your advice. And exactly what I thought would happen, happened. My wife thought I was nuts and just played along with it. Overall, she thinks it's annoying that I keep calling her and repeating the same speech. And how am I supposed to sound like I mean it, when I really don't?"

I sighed. "Okay, I understand. But I need you to try it for two more weeks. And this time, I want you to give it your all, even if your wife seems to be pushing you away while you are reading it. I want you to read the list slowly and carefully to her and try to envision those first months or years when you *did* feel that way about her, and *did* think about those qualities."

"You just don't give up, do you? Okay, whatever," he said and slammed down the phone. As angry as he was, I knew he was going to try it.

Two weeks later, I got a phone call, and this time it was a very different type of call. It was the magical phone call I was hoping for. "You won't believe this, Yisroel! I actually started to mean the things I was saying! And Rebecca could tell in my voice that things had changed. And she in turn, started to reciprocate with saying the qualities that she really loved about me. We started laughing and sharing more, and the spark that we once had started to come back! We now joke around about the scheduled time when we give each other our pep talk about the things we like about each other! And it also helped me to realize that it isn't just the qualities that I love about her, I just love her for who she is, independent of the qualities!"

I beamed. I was hoping for this, and his words were certainly music to my ears. "That is wonderful! Now it is time to move on to Phase Two. Before you begin to work on Phase Two, you need to once again repeat the qualities you really love about her. Phase Two is talking about the things she does that upset you and asking if she could try to be more considerate for your need, like having a little more time to relax after a long stressful day at work. And she in turn could speak to you about the things she really feel she needs. You aren't trying to *change* her, you are just trying to change some of her daily routine that is really upsetting you. And in turn, she can speak to you about the things that are really upsetting her, and to see if you can accommodate her. Again, she isn't going to try to *change* you, just change some habits that are upsetting her. But please make sure to butter each other up with the good qualities you like in each other first!"

He smiled, "You know, for a single guy, you really seem to know a lot about marriage! Where do you get your ideas from?"

"It is very simple. I get it from *davening*. This is how we talk to God every day. We begin the *Amidah* by praising God and talking about His infinite power and wisdom. We talk about the goodness He bestows to the world, and that He sustains every living creature. Only then, do we begin talking about our wants and needs, health, wisdom, financial success, redemption, etc. It is always important to recognize and speak about how dependent we know we are on Him and how we need His help to get us through the day."

He grinned again and shook his head, "*Oy vey*! Here you go again with the spiritual stuff!"

"Well, this stuff works!" I said, "In so many ways, our spiritual lives mirror our physical lives. Just try it, and report back in a month, okay?"

He took my advice and sure enough it worked. He said they both started to be more sensitive to the other person's needs and started to change some of their habits to accommodate each other. There were still some rough patches, but overall things were great, and their marriage spark was once again renewed. They have been happily married ever since.

I don't take any credit for what happened between them. I was just chosen as the *shaliach* (messenger) and it was God who put the right words in my mouth at the right time. I am grateful that for whatever reason, I was chosen to give Adam this message.

Prayer as a Vehicle to Transform Ourselves

Herein lies the problem that makes prayer so hard, but also to what makes prayer so much more meaningful. It is all about one thing, and that is building within ourselves a love and relationship to God and using words as the vehicle to develop this love. We often think that love needs to preempt the words of love that we say, but often it is the other way around. Words lead to feeling and action as well. At first it the words may seem empty and as if one is just "going through the motions" but eventually it can become very real. The words can then become a part of you. But this takes a tremendous amount of work. This is why prayer is referred to as work. But that is when it becomes the most meaningful, after the work has been put in, and the words become real.

There is a statement in *Pirkei Avot*, "Nullify your will before His Will, so that He will nullify His Will before your will." I believe this passage hints to this idea. Prayer is not merely *asking for things, it is realignment of our wants and needs*. It is the process of often changing our will to His will, to remembering what is most important in life. And, as discussed in the prelude to the book when we discussed reaching our potential, we have the ability to become much greater people when we pray for we are latching on to a Force much greater than ourselves, and thereby yearning for things much greater than our mere physical bodies. Only then, do our prayers have a much greater chance of being answered with the outcome we desire. Abraham Joshua Heschel put it most succinctly, "Prayer takes the mind out of the narrowness of self-interest, and enables us to see the world in the mirror of the holy. For when we betake ourselves to the extreme opposite of the ego, we can behold a situation from the aspect of God."

I remember reading a parable that Rebbetzin Esther Jungreis once wrote. She talked about a Prince of Darkness who looked hideous and his actions mirrored his appearance. He cursed, insulted, and often fought with anyone who crossed his path. One day, he saw a beautiful young maiden walking by, and he desired her very much. But he could tell she had a sweet innocence to her and would never be attracted to his appearance and actions. So he went to the best mask-maker in the village and asked him to make a mask of a very handsome man. He put it on, and went to meet her. Around her, he put on the persona of a charming sensitive and sweet individual. It was very difficult for him to put on such a persona, but he knew he loved her and this something he knew he must do. Eventually he won her hand in marriage. Years went by and he kept up the façade, never removing the mask and never revealing his inner character. Somehow, one day, the mask-maker saw him. Upset that the Prince had put on the ruse for so long, he went over and ripped the mask off of his face. And lo and behold! The face underneath exactly mirrored the face on the mask! All of the years of going through the motions of wearing both the physical mask and the mask of his actions and words had penetrated his soul. And now he really *was* the person he was pretending to be! It was no longer an act; it became who he now truly was. And he had now become a person much greater than he ever was.

So it is with our relationship with God. I believe it is even harder because we don't see God, we only see Him through the world around us. So it is harder to always feel that closeness to him the way we may feel around our spouse or our children. This is why prayer isn't a simple exercise that we do just for a month, like I told my friend Adam. It is an exercise that we do for a lifetime.

And only once we begin to feel this love and how much we truly need Him, do we begin to feel we can ask Him for the things we need. And even in the things we ask Him, we are also still working on ourselves, for we are recalibrating many of our wants and needs. We don't ask start off by asking God for money so we can go on the best vacation, or buy the fanciest car. We start by asking Him for the things that really truly matter the most, like wisdom, health, forgiveness, and redemption both in our personal lives and in our national lives. We pray not to be swayed by false ideologies. We pray for the return to Zion and Jerusalem. Even when we pray for financial freedom, it is to help support ourselves and our families, but not to indulge in every luxury that comes our way. So in this way, even what we ask for requires work on our part, since it takes effort to realign our wants and needs with what is truly what is best for us.

This is why Faith can only come after love. Love must precede faith, because only when we love someone can we begin to develop trust that the person will always be there for us and will try to help us succeed in living our lives to the fullest. This is the difference between blind faith and faith with vision. Blind faith is when there is faith before any established love, and it is little more than a shot in the dark. It is like walking through a dark maze and somehow hoping to come out the other side. But faith with vision is faith with love, which is like walking through the same maze but this time holding the hand of an experienced guide.

There is a statement in the Talmud that if one is praying and he or she is not being answered, a person should strengthen himself or herself and pray again. The Talmud brings the following verse from the book of Psalms, "Hope to God, strengthen yourself and He will give you courage. Hope to God." The repetition of the words, "Hope to God," tells us if at first prayer doesn't seem to work, to strengthen one's heart and try prayer again. I believe the emphasis here is on *strengthening one's heart.* This means trying as best as one can to fill oneself with an awareness of our love for God and how much we need Him to help us in our lives. It takes tremendous work, and indeed strengthening one's heart to overcome any sense of apathy. And once again, begin to pray anew. We see this from the well, known story of Choni Ha-Ma'agil, Choni the Circle-Maker. The story took place during a terrible drought. Choni drew a circle and prayed to God, and said to Him he would not leave the circle until it started to rain. And miraculously, it did in fact, start to rain. Although Choni demonstrated perhaps a bit of *chutzpah*, in reality he was also demonstrating how much he knew full well that Him, and only Him can do the impossible. Only He could bring much rain during a terrible drought. Only He can help us with what we want and need.

Prayer as a Way to See Our Connection to God

I believe some of the work of prayer involves something even greater. There is an incredible passage in the Talmud; the Talmud discusses why King David said *Borchi nafshi et Hashem*, "my soul praises God," on five different occasions. What did these five times symbolize? The Talmud explains that they are five ways in which the soul is similar to God:

1. Just as God fills the entire universe, so too our soul fills our entire body.

2. Just as God sees, but is not seen, so too our soul sees but is not seen.

3. Just as God nourishes the entire world, so too our soul nourishes our body.

4. Just as God is pure, so too our soul is pure.

5. Just as God resides in the innermost chambers, so too our soul resides there as well.

The Talmud concluded with an affirming statement, "Let the one who possesses these five attributes give praise to the One who possesses these attributes."

This idea is a very powerful one indeed, for I believe it lies at the core of what we are hoping to accomplish with prayer. It isn't just that we are *praising Him,* we are *recognizing that we are a part of Him and He is a part of us.* This is the greatest testament to true love, to recognize one as being totally intimately bound to one another, to being cut from the same cloth, so to speak. This indeed takes a lot of work, for indeed we don't see the soul, much as we don't see God. But that is where the work begins, and when true love begins to blossom.

What has helped me in the past to pray with more feeling is to pray through song. We all know there is a very strong link between the world of prayer, and the world of the melody. One of my favorite passages in the Talmud is expounding on a verse in the Prophets, "To listen unto the song and onto prayer." The Talmud explains that in a place where there is song, there is prayer. Real song can bring one to pray, and real prayer can bring one to sing. King David, the author of Psalms, who once declared in his writing *Ani Tefillah*, "I am prayer," was also known as the sweet singer of Israel who had written many beautiful melodies and used a harp to sing his praises. This path was continued by the Baal Shem Tov, and it has seen a resurgence in our time, especially with the melodies of Shlomo Carlebach. We see throughout the Psalms themselves how much it important to praise God through song and instrument, "Praise Him with lyre and harp, praise Him with drum and dance, praise Him with organ and flute, praise Him with clanging cymbals, praise Him with resonant trumpets." Even outside of the book of Psalms it writes in our prayer, "Master of Worlds who chooses songs of prayer." Through singing, our prayers take on a whole new layer of meaning.

My blessing to everyone is to gain a greater understanding and appreciation of prayer in general, and be able to use it as a springboard for self growth and introspection. And may all of our prayers be answered favorably.

Spiritual Exercises

1. Try to remember a time when praying made a profound impact on you. What were you praying for? How did you feel toward God during that time? How did you feel toward your own life?

2. Next time you pray for something, try to make a mental picture of what you are praying for as you are saying the prayer.

3. Next time you pray, during the parts of prayer that are the most crucial try to sing the words softly to yourself with you favorite spiritual melody. Take note how this affects your prayers from that point on.

4. Try to take a few minutes before prayer and mentally prepare yourself. Turn off your cell phone, go to a quiet area, relax, and contemplate the beauty of the words you are about to say. Then make a chronicle of how this simple exercise changes your prayer and your life in general.

5. Try to get in the habit of praying from a Siddur (prayer book). Praying from a Siddur can enhance one's concentration on the words, and help prevent stumbling on the words.

Chapter 8
Renewal & Redemption

Once Rabbi Hiyya the Great and Rabbi Shimon Bar Halafta were taking a stroll together in the Arbel Valley to the west of the sea of Galilee, at the break of dawn. They saw the first rays of light breaking over the horizon. Rabbi Hiyya the Great said to Rabbi Shimon Bar Halafta: "Thus will the redemption of Israel be. It will materialize gradually come to the surface, as the verse indicates, 'As I sit in darkness, God is my light.' At first it will come little by little, and then it will gradually shimmer, and then it will be fruitful and multiply, and then- it will spread out and around."

~ Song of Songs Rabbah

M Y FRIENDS, WE ARE LIVING in incredible times. The Zohar teaches us that in the era of the Messiah the world will be very small, and very short. One hundred years ago, this statement seemed to have very little meaning. But in our times, the statement is all too clear. Our age has been different than any other times in history. The world has indeed become very small. In addition, projects that would have taken years to develop in the past can now be done at a much quicker speed, sometimes even in hours or minutes.

We have reaped the glowing profits of what technology has wrought for us, we can now place a phone call to anywhere in the world or hear thousands of songs with tiny devices that sit in our pockets. We can send photos, documents, programs, with the click of a few buttons. Medical science has changed our world dramatically. One can merely pop a pill for a variety of ailments; people can now live longer with artificial supports. The human heart can be replicated by human hands enough to sustain one's life. We can fly nearly anywhere in the world in a matter of hours. The spiritual realm has changed dramatically as well with the technological boom. Now, Torah lectures can be watched, words of Torah can be emailed, downloaded, and printed from any teacher in the world. There is even an iPod which has the entire Talmud contained in it. Virtual libraries with thousands of holy books are at one's disposal with just a click of a few buttons.

On the other hand, technology has magnified the dangers in the world. Entire nations have experienced genocide and the era of global terrorism has reared its ugly head. Hitler's Nazi atrocities, Al Qaeda and the terrorist attacks of September 11, 2001, the endless violence of Hamas and the Second Intifada, and Saddam Hussein's attempts at genocide, have shown us the potential horrors that technology can wreak if misused. The threat of nuclear holocaust remains a stark possibility in the face of mad dictators possessing weapons of mass destruction. And totalitarian regimes can spread propaganda and hatred to the masses with relative ease. The world of impurity has been strengthened as well. Pornography can be downloaded with the click of a button; forbidden chat rooms can be accessed by nearly all.

Technology has also made the world increasingly more complex. Noise is louder, traffic is longer, and people are getting more busy and impatient. People expect more, and demand more comforts.

I have always been fascinated by the following verse, "And the hearts of the fathers will turn toward their sons, and the hearts of their sons will turn toward their fathers." We see over and over again in our times how the older generation sees the speed and complexity of the new generation and the many spiritual benefits and knowledge that comes with the new modern age. And the young generation looks up to the old, sees the beauty of their tradition and faith, what their years and life experiences have taught them. I remember once hearing a photographer say that a good photographer doesn't try to take out the wrinkles in a man's face with Photoshop; he keeps the wrinkles in, for every wrinkle tells a story. Indeed, what we can learn from our elders and from previous generation is vast and deep. This is especially true with the generation who went through the Holocaust and was able to emerge not only with their faith intact, but at times even strengthened; a generation who experienced immeasurable suffering but also experienced the miraculous and historical return to the Land of our Fathers.

Moreover, on an individual level, we live in an almost constant state of confusion. There are more opportunities for instant gratification than ever before; we have lived through the sexual revolution, as well as countless forms of entertainment with the click of a button. And yet, we are a generation that is depressed and anxious. We have been dubbed "The Prozac Nation" as more people than ever before have turned to prescription medications, as well as psychotherapy, self-help books and lectures. Incidence of suicide, sadly enough, continues to climb. Many turn to illegal narcotics in an effort to end their pain.

What does it all mean? Is the world heading toward perfection, or toward destruction? What are the answers? Are there answers?

The only choice we are given in life is to turn to the one source book God has provided us, the manual on how to lead our lives; the Torah. We are taught by the Sages "Turn it and turn it, for all is contained in it." What does the Torah say about the uniqueness of our generation? What does it all mean?

Darkness Precedes Light

King Solomon wrote in the Song of Songs, "When I lay down to sleep at night, I seek the love of my soul, but I cannot find him. I arise and wander through the cities and marketplaces, I am seeking the love of my soul." Most of the commentators say the Song of Songs is an allegory of the love of God and His People. This verse is a reference to the long exile, which is compared to night. Why is exile compared to night? One may say we have all the comforts we can ask for! One need only press a button, and the world is opened up before him. The Internet, cell phones, and television have radically changed our world. One may be sitting in the comfort of their own home, but part of them is somewhere else. There is a part of them which is ensconced in whatever pleasure, fantasy or conversation they are in. Is this exile really so bitter?

The answer to this question is very revealing, not only to further elucidate the verse in Song of Songs, but to teach us what exile really is and what we are lacking. Nighttime, as we all know does not serve any purpose, except that it is the time to rejuvenate our bodies for the next day. It is the day which is really the focal point of our lives, for that is the time when we are the most productive. Sleep is necessary to fuel us for the energy we use to reach our daily goals. In the morning we pray, "We gratefully acknowledge before you that you are the living King for all eternity who has returned our souls to us. When we are asleep, our souls leave us for the spiritual rejuvenation needed for the next day. Not only in the spiritual realm do we need this rejuvenation, bit our bodies need it as well.

What does this mean? This means that this premessianic world, with all of its lures and pleasures, is still only the night preparing for the day. It is not the ideal state that our soul needs to be most productive. The real state that our souls need is what it will experience when we are fully awake, when the Great Day will come. When we arise in the morning, we recite the blessing, "Blessed is the Lord who has given us understanding to discern the difference between day and night." What sort of blessing is this? Doesn't every living thing know the difference between day and night? Is this something to really bless God for? Rabbi Moshe Weinberger explains so beautifully that this simple, seemingly mundane blessing is really touching this profound principle: *real wisdom means understanding the difference between this world and the messianic world.* Real wisdom means knowing that this world is still transient. The same way we say this prayer just after we wake up in the morning, so too we must remember that deep inner truth which we so often deny or forget, but at times we are forced to confront.

Another difference between night and day is the ability to see. When it is dark, our vision is not so clear. At night, a darkened path may cause us to stumble. However, when it is day, we can see the path in front of us very clearly. The pre-messianic world is the world of darkness which precedes the light. Only when the messiah comes we will understand this world.

Rabbi Weinberger continues and explains that this is why in Judaism, the night precedes the day. All of our holidays and the Sabbath begin at sundown the night before. This is derived from the Biblical verse in the beginning of Genesis, "And it was evening, and it was morning, one day." The verse mentions evening first since that is the order of what constitutes a "day." The order of our history will also mimic the order of creation. Darkness always precedes the light; the night must come before we can experience the day. The exile is just the prelude to the coming days of the messiah.

The Struggle of Good and Evil

We see this concept most succinctly from the Bible story of Jacob wrestling the angel of Esau. In Genesis it is written about a mysterious confrontation between our Patriarch Jacob and the angel of his nemesis Esau. Esau, as we know from the Biblical story, was greedy, lustful, and violent. His angel represents the lures of this physical world, and its many trappings and pitfalls. Jacob represents simplicity, truth, and purity, namely the world after the messiah. Therefore, this wrestling match takes on mystical proportions. It is very significant that this struggle to place at night. For when it was dark, Jacob was being tested. The stakes were very high, for before Jacob can confront his twin brother Esau, he must confront the symbolic Esau, the Esau inside of him. At night, the truth becomes unclear, and what is real may not appear to be. When the dawn came, Jacob emerged from the confrontation victorious. Dawn is likened to the era of the messiah, as the *Midrash* says, "The Jewish People will be redeemed like the sun slowly rising and spreading its rays over the horizon." In the verse it is written, "Jacob was left alone, he wrestled the man until dawn." The Sages connect this verse mystically to a verse in Isaiah which is uses similar wording. The prophet writes, "On that Day, God will be exalted alone." This verse refers to the messianic era. Here we see the link between dawn and night, the world before the messiah and after the messiah.

This is why it is written in the verse, "I will remember My covenant with Jacob, and also My covenant with Isaac, and My covenant with Abraham, and I will remember the Land." Here, Rashi points out that Jacob is mentioned first, since this verse is an illusion to the coming of the Messiah, and it will be Jacob who will herald it. Furthermore, Rashi writes that there are five times when the Torah writes *Yaakov* (the Hebrew name for Jacob) with the Hebrew letter *vav* and there are five times when the name *Eliyahu* (the Hebrew name for Elijah) without a *vav*. What does this mean? Rashi writes that Jacob, so to speak, took as collateral the "vav" from Elijah's name to ensure that there will one day be redemption. Elijah, the mystical figure, who never really died, is the prophet who is with us in exile, and will be there to greet us when the Messiah comes. Here is the deep connection between Elijah and Jacob, their partnership in our People's destiny. It is written, "Behold I will send you Elijah the prophet, before you on the Day of God, the great and awesome Day." The prophet Elijah and the patriarch Jacob stand with us in exile and will be with us in redemption as well.

One thing is for certain, modern times and the freedoms that ensues from it, has caused a greater existential struggle than at any other time in our history. The Baal Shem Tov taught us that in the days before the Messiah, there will be similar struggles to what occurred in Biblical times in the days of the Flood and the Tower. In the Torah, it is written, "The entire earth was filled with corruption." We have seen in our times not only an unprecedented level of greed and immorality, but also an acceptance, an even sometimes an encouragement of such behavior. And the episode of the Tower of Babel bears even closer resemblance to our generation. That generation sought to "reach the Heavens by building a great tower, and fight God." As ridiculous as that may sound to our modern ears, in many way we are building our own "towers" and trying to remove God from our world. Technology, especially with the explosions in communication has led to an incredible sense of arrogance, as well as a coldness, or distance from God. It has caused many to *feel* as if we no longer need God, and God no longer cares for us. We bow and worship our laptops, our cell phones, our iPods, etc. The generation of the Tower is called in Hebrew *haflagah,* which means "separation." Indeed, the people sought to create a separation between ourselves and God. I think of this when I see people on their cell phones during prayer services. We are a generation constantly trying to *escape*, rather than pause and *reflect*.

Our Personal Redemption

To prepare ourselves for Redemption, we need to go through our own personal redemption. This has many ramifications, first and foremost, it means understanding that the world as we know it, is still in an incomplete state. As much as Torah has proliferated, as much as more Jews are returning to their roots, and the world as a whole has been seeking more and more a deeper sense of spirituality, is still not what it will be when the Messiah comes. The Messiah will usher in a new era, in some ways similar to our own, and in some ways vastly different that the world we know. So to redeem ourselves on a personal level means longing each and every day for a different and better world than the one we know. It means giving up some our materialistic pursuits and values, and yearning for a more spiritual existence.

In the previous century, the late Lubavitcher Rebbe stood up to the world and taught this to his Chassidim in every one of his teachings. Some people believe that the Rebbe himself was the long awaited Messiah. I believe this to be a misunderstanding of the Rebbe and his message. He was there to teach us fundamentally this great principle: prepare yourself each day for the long awaited Messiah and help bring the world to a place where it is ready to receive him.

The Sages tell us that there are three leaders who will ride a donkey. The Hebrew word for donkey is *chamor,* which comes from the same word as *chomer*, which means matter, or physicality. By writing that these three leaders rode *on top* of the donkey is telling us that these people showed their mastery over the physical world. This is the ultimate triumph of spirituality, to have complete control over physicality. These three people are Abraham, Moses, and the Messiah. What is the significance of these three? All of them were born into challenging circumstances. Abraham stood up against a savage pagan world and declared there is one God, and the world is built on kindness, faith, and morality. Moses, born and raised by the Pharaoh, and yet was able to reject it and become the ultimate spiritual conduit who gave us the Torah. And finally, there is the Messiah, who will come into a world with great explosions in materialism and temptations, and yet will eventually triumph over it. The era of the Messiah is the ultimate triumph of the soul, as the prophets write, "Behold, days are coming, says God, when the world will be hungry and thirsty, but not thirsty for water and not hungry for bread, but to hear the word of God." We are living in the dichotomy to proceed these days; the struggle goes on every waking moment of our lives. We see the explosions of technology and its harmful effects, but we have also seen the same technology to create a rebirth of Torah and the burning desire to hear His word.

The Physical World Parallels the Spiritual World

The word *Kabbalah* comes from the root word *kabel,* which means "receive." However, there is another meaning; it also comes from the root word *makbil*, which means 'parallel." This means that in many ways the cycle of life in the physical world parallels the cycle of life in the spiritual world. Just when the world seems destroyed and barren from the winter, spring comes and the earth experiences rebirth. When a caterpillar goes into its cocoon seemingly to wither away, what emerges is a butterfly, a creature much more beautiful and capable than what it was before. In a human life, there is the miracle of birth, the cycle of life through marriage, child-rearing, and the cycle of life begins again.

In the spiritual world, there are cycles as well, many with the number seven. There is the cycle of the seven days of the week, there is the seven years of the *shemitah* cycle relating to our fields, and there is the cycle of seven for the millennium of time. We are taught in the Talmud that the seventh millennium will be a period of Rest, the Era of the Messiah, just like the seventh day is the day of rest for the week and the seventh year is the year of rest for the field. And much like in the physical world, it is precisely when all seems lost and destroyed that what emerges is something much greater and different than what was before. The Era of the Messiah will be a very different world than the world we know of now. Much like the butterfly that emerges from the cocoon, the Era of the Messiah will radiate with spiritual beauty, an era of peace and tranquility.

The mystics teach us that the messianic era will be a transition into a new state of consciousness. We all know of the ram's horn, known as the Shofar, which we blow every Rosh Hashanah, and at the end of Yom Kippur as we transition from a state of impurity into purity. The ram's horn is symbolic of the ram which was offered by Abraham on the altar instead of Isaac. It was at that moment that Abraham became the Father of a new nation, as he demonstrated his everlasting faith in God and passed the final test given to him by God. Where do we see the blowing of the Shofar in the Torah? There are two times that the great Shofar was blown in the Torah, once in our past and once in the future. Once occurred at the giving of the Torah, when we transitioned from a group of recently freed slaves into a Chosen People who were given a Divine Purpose. The second time will be in our future when the Prophets write a great Shofar will be blown again, signifying the beginning of a new era. All of these ideas signify a time of great change, a time of rebirth. When the Messiah will come, the world will be a very different place. There will be a transition, there will be a new awareness of God that doesn't exist today.

Preparing Ourselves for the Messiah

So how do we even begin to prepare for the great and imminent Day? The answer is quite simple, yet so difficult. It begins with us. Each person needs to prepare for the Redemption by rectifying themselves. Each person contains a microcosm of human history within them. Each person has experienced the enormous vicissitudes of life that history has experienced on a global level. We have all experienced at some point in our lives suffering, pain, loss, poverty and illness. We have also experienced joy, triumph, laughter, and contentment. On a global level, the world has seen earthquakes, war, terrorism, hurricanes, famine, theft, and murder. At the same time, world history has experienced joy, charity, unity, and peace. We have seen countries rebuilt that have once been destroyed. And the emotional struggles we experience on a personal level are also experienced on a cosmic level as well. Every person at some point in their life experiences struggles with melancholy, prejudice, sadness, as well as anger and aggression. Human history has also struggled with these emotions.

And so it must be; that as the world slowly begins to herald the arrival of the Messiah, the only way to prepare for it is by trying to perfect ourselves. When one contributes to others on a personal level, he or she is contributing on a cosmic level as well. One can only begin to prepare for the arrival of the Messiah when one realizes that his or her life is sorely lacking. The imperfections that we see on a global level apply on an individual level as well. We experience imperfections in our lives all the time. Even when we experience the joys of living, such as a wedding or the birth of a new child, or a materialistic pleasure such as a vacation or relaxing in a spa, one can still feel a sense of lacking. One may still often feel that as great as these joys are, perhaps there is a joy even greater. Perhaps there is a joy which is *eternal*. When one experiences that feeling of *wanting* something even more, something which the world in the present state that it is in does not have, then one has begun to yearn for the coming of the Messiah. And certainly when one experiences the darker side of life's journeys, the loss of a loved one, a divorce, serious illness, or the loss of a job, then one experiences this yearning even more. This *can't* be all that life has to offer. There must be a brighter Day coming.

Yearning for the Messiah

This is why believing and *yearning* for the Messiah is so paramount to Jewish Faith. It is one of the thirteen principles of Maimonides, "I believe in the coming of the Messiah, and even though he may tarry, nevertheless, every day I await his coming." It is discussed throughout our prayers on a daily basis. In fact, every prayer ends with *Alenu,* which is all about the time of Redemption, as it says, "Idols will be destroyed, false gods will be cut away, and the world will be fixed with the Kingdom of the Almighty." These are powerful and important words, words that deserve to be reiterated after every prayer. For through these prayers we realize our world is in an incomplete state. We realize how badly we need the world to be fixed, how yearning for Redemption gives us a sense of hope, a sense of renewal. It is a yearning to once again connect with our God, and to usher in a new era of closeness to Him. It is the yearning that the bride and groom have for each other before their wedding, when they will be joined together as one. When one begins to feel this yearning, true love begins to blossom. For love begins when a person realizes he or she cannot bear to be apart from the other. It is the yearning of the verse in Habakkuk writes, "The knowledge of the glory of God will fill the earth as the water fills the sea." May we all merit seeing this Great Day come. May we all live to see the rebuilding of Jerusalem and the return to Zion in our days.

Spiritual Exercises

1. Try to remember a time when you yearned for a different world than the one we are currently in. What was it that upset you about our world? What did you want to be different about it?

2. What do you think will the physical world be like when the Messiah comes? Will we still be living where we are now? Will there be illness? Wars? Famine? Poverty? Natural disasters?

3. What do you think the spiritual world will be like when the Messiah comes? Will people be yearning for a more Godly life? Will there be more Torah study and prayer? What will be of other religions? Will people have less materialistic pursuits or feel the need for materialistic wealth?

4. Try to take a few minutes out of each day and pray for the coming of the Messiah. During that time, try to think about what you feel the world will look like when the Messiah comes. Then chronicle how your day and your life change after this activity.

Chapter 9
Looking for Love in All the Right Places

A woman of valor, who can find? Far beyond pearls is her value. Her husband's heart relies on her and she lacks no fortune. She repays his good, but never his harm, all the days of her life.

~ Proverbs 31

IT IS THE SUBJECT OF nearly every pop song, every movie, every novel, and countless numbers of poems and philosophy books. People talk about it constantly, it is the subject of talk shows, therapy sessions, and is on our minds constantly. Yet as discussed as it is, people are at a loss to really describe it, or let alone define it. The subject, of course, is Love. Love takes on many forms. It is the love between siblings, a parent to a child, a child to a parent, or best friends. But the Love discussed most is the love between man and woman. This unique love will be the subject of this chapter.

It is interesting to note that perhaps the most discussed subject in the world somehow eludes definition. And yet everyone who has experienced it, somehow say it is the most real thing they have ever experienced. It reminds me of a quote I once saw that said, "the most real things in the world are not 'things' at all. Compassion, Kindness, Inspiration, and Spirituality are not "things." And Love is most certainly not a "thing" and yet we know how real it is.

Rabbi Akiva Tatz writes a beautiful insight into why the world is so obsessed with Love. Nearly everything we do in life is work; we are constantly looking forward to a result. However, what gives us the most satisfaction in life isn't the process of Running; it is the process of Arriving. Even the most wonderful journey in the world doesn't compare to finally reaching the desired destination. Love is the ultimate experience of having arrived, of finally finding what one has been seeking for so long. In fact, the Torah uses the word "find" when describing marriage, "When a man *finds* a woman to marry." Many people describe the experience of finding one's soul mate as finding something that was once lost, in fact the spouse seems familiar to them, as if they had once known him or her long ago. There is no greater joy in the world than to finally at long last no longer need to seek, but to revel in the serenity of having found and discovered. It is the feeling of coming home after a long time away.

So who in society knows the most about love? I always find it ironic that the people who we think should know the most about love often in reality seem to know the least. Most of the people who sing the love songs on the radio, write novels about love, or act in romantic comedies, people who are surrounded by "love themes," often have the most dysfunctional personal lives. Brief marriages, bitter divorces, custody battles, affairs, restraining orders, the list goes on. So clearly the most "famous" people who talk about love are not the people who really know the most about it. Until recently, this was the chapter I always wanted to write, but didn't feel I was equipped well enough to write it. After all, I was a single guy, who was I to comment on love between man and woman? Would someone read a chapter about how beautiful the Grand Canyon is from someone who never visited it? But now that I have finally met the special someone who I want to share the rest of my life with, I feel a little better equipped to comment on it. Not an overnight expert, but at least I have an inkling of what it is.

What Love Is

Real Love is something that takes years to develop, years of giving and sharing. One of my favorite quotes is, "A happy man marries the girl he loves, but a happier man loves the girl he marries." It is the lifetime together *after* the marriage, *not* the act of getting married that makes the Love real. It is interesting to note in the Torah that in one of the very first marriages in the Torah it writes, "Isaac married Rebecca and then he loved her." Why the order of marriage, and *only then* love? For it is this very same idea, real love only comes *after* marriage, after commitment; after giving and communicating in a loving long term relationship.

This idea reminds me of the famous story once told over by Stephen Covey, the author of *The Seven Habit of Highly Effective People*. A man once approached him about marriage difficulties and said that he no longer is "in love" with his wife. Mr. Covey answered him tersely, "Okay, then start loving her." The man was confused, and repeated again that he was not "in love" with his wife anymore. Mr. Covey again said that he should now begin to *love* her, meaning love is not a *noun*, it is a *verb*. It is an act that we do when we give, when we share, and when we commit.

The Jewish View on Love

What are Judaism's views on Love? Is it a fundamental of Torah and Jewish belief? How does it differ from society's views on Love?

We find some clues to the Torah's view on Love right at the beginning of the Torah. The Torah describes Adam's loneliness and writes, "it is not good for man to be alone." Each individual was created as an incomplete being, and each person searches tirelessly for that other half. The Torah describes Eve, as a "rib" that was taken from Adam and fashioned into a woman. There is even a well-known *Midrash* that Adam and Eve were created as one androgynous being and then separated into two. Whether or not this *Midrash* or this "rib" was meant to be taken literally, it certainly contains a serious truth. Without the fulfillment of a loving partner by our side, one is in a constant state of searching, of feeling incomplete, as if a part was taken and is missing. When a man and woman stand under the sacred canopy of marriage—the *chuppah*—as soul-mates, there is the sense of joy, of finally reconnecting, and finding what has been missing for so long.

I believe Judaism isn't just concerned about Love, it is obsessed with Love. One of my favorite titles of a book is Rabbi David Aaron's, *Love is my Religion*. Nearly every prayer we utter talks about the special love we have for God and appreciating His goodness both to the world and in our own personal lives. For it is our love that is at the forefront of everything, it is what makes us want to serve and get close to God, it propels us to keep His *mitzvot* and care for our fellow man. And of course it is Love that is what propels us to give and care for our significant others.

The Talmud relates a fascinating dialogue between a Sage, a heretic, and the heretic's daughter. The story is as follows:

A heretic said to the Sage, "Your God is a thief! For it is written in Scripture 'The Lord God cast a deep sleep on Adam, and he slept, and God took one of his sides… and He fashioned the side… into a woman.' We see that God stole Adam's side!"

The heretic's daughter said to the Sage, "Leave my father alone, for I will answer him." She turned to her father and said, "Give me a judge who can exact justice for me." The heretic asked, "What do you want a judge for?" His daughter responded, "Thieves came upon is in the night and they took from us a silver pitcher and left us a golden pitcher in its place." He said to her incredulously, "If only such thieves were to come upon us every day!" She answered, "So it was with Adam. It is true that one side was taken from him, but can't you see what was given back to him in its place! He was given helpmate to support him with all of his endeavors."

This is the great gift that God has given to man; he has taken away a silver pitcher only to replace it with a golden one. A woman has the ability to give man the confidence, physical and moral support he needs to reach the greatest potential that he possibly can. She can lift up her husband when he is down, she can bring joy into his life, and she can provide him with children, self worth, love, and dignity.

There is a parable in the *Midrash* to this idea. The *Midrash* writes that once a very righteous, holy couple unfortunately decided to get divorced. The husband then went and married a really bitter, rotten woman. As time went by, unfortunately this once holy person became embittered and disgusting as well. In the meantime, the wife married someone who was also disgusting and coarse. However, with time, she was able to soften him and change him till he too became holy and righteous. Rabbi Moshe Weinberger says that we see from this portion that a woman has the *power to create a new person*, to turn a wicked person into a righteous person. She can plant seeds of goodness into a vessel that was once a barren wasteland, bereft of redeeming qualities.

It goes without saying that the opposite can be true as well, as many couples can attest. A husband can empower his wife to bring out the best in her, to help her bring her own dreams to fruition, to give her love and companionship. However, this ability to create, to build, is best accomplished by a woman, for her soft nurturing qualities, and kind loving words can help bring her husband to his ultimate potential. This is seen from King Solomon's Book of Proverbs when he writes, "She opens her mouth with wisdom, and a teaching of kindness is on her tongue." This is the unique power that a woman has.

A Helpmate Who Opposes Him

One of the greatest lessons about this incredible potential that a woman has can be seen with from the very beginning of the Torah in the Book of Genesis. After God created Adam the verse writes, "I shall make a helpmate opposite him." Many of the commentators are puzzled by this expression, for how can a woman be a helpmate if she is opposite him, meaning opposing him?

Two of the great commentators write a great deal about this: Rabbi Naftali Tzevi Yehudah of Berlin (the *Netziv*), and the Ishbitzer Rebbe, a Chassidic Master. They write that there are times when a wife can oppose her husband and really be helping him, and there are times when a wife can support her husband and really be destroying him. For example, let us say that a man comes home one day from a long hard day of work. He spends twenty minutes at the dinner table ranting about how horrible his boss is and how he wishes his boss would either quit his job or get fired so he would never have to see him again. His wife agrees with him and supports him by continuing his tirade against his boss. What will happen when his anger dissolves? He will realize that his wife is bringing out the worst in him by encouraging his anger and bitterness!

On the other hand, what would happen if his wife opposes him and says that maybe his boss isn't so bad, maybe he has some redeeming qualities like nearly everyone does, and he may be going through something difficult that is causing him to act this way? At first, undoubtedly he will be angry at his wife for saying this and for not supporting him. But how will he feel when his anger dissipates? He will realize that his wife is truly extraordinary, that she brings out the best in him and causes him to see the goodness inside of everyone.

I saw this in my own personal life when I got engaged to my wife. Before and during the engagement, I was terrified of the idea of committing myself to just one person. After so many years of dating, I had grown used to the *search* and not to the *goal*. I kept thinking, "Well, maybe there will be someone *else* with an even stronger and better connection and attraction," and I frantically wanted (or least *thought* I wanted) to re-renter the prospect of searching yet again. But my wife stood fast and continuously prevented me from running away from her and gave me strong words of encouragement that we were right for each other. There were times I was upset at her from resisting me, from blocking me from what I perceived as my ticket to freedom. But I realized in reality she wasn't *hurting* me, she was *helping* me. She was pulling me out of a lifetime of frustration, a never ending rat race without an end in sight, all the while getting more lonely, depressed and bitter with each passing year. By her opposing me, she wasn't really *stifling* me, she was really *saving* me.

This concept of helpful opposition can be seen in the biblical story of Korach, who rebelled against Moses, accused him of arrogance, and tried to instigate the people to follow him instead of Moses. The Talmud tells us what Korach's wife said to him. It writes:

When God said to Moses, "Take the Levites from among the Jewish People and purify them... Let them

151

pass a razor over their entire flesh," he immediately did so to Korach... Korach's wife said to him: Look what Moses did to you! He became the king; his brother he made the High Priest; his nephews he made [regular] priests. When *terumah* is brought, he says it should be for the priest. When tithes are brought, he says, give one-tenth to the priest. But for you, he shaves your hair, ridicules you and belittles you!

Here words eventually led to Korach rebelling against Moses. Here was an example of a woman who supported her husband, yet at the same time she was appealing to his worst elements; jealousy, power, and greed. Although she was supporting her husband, she was in fact, destroying him.

However, within the same story we find the opposite as well. The Talmud tells us about a person named On son of Pelet, one of the rebels in Korach's mutiny. However, his wife dissuaded him. The story is as follows:

She said to him, "What will you gain from this? If Moses prevails, you will be a mere follower, and if Korach prevails, you will remain just a follower." He said to her, "What shall I do? I was with them in the plan, and I swore to them that if they call me, I will go with them." She said to him, "Stay home, and I will save you." She gave him wine to drink so he would fall asleep. She sat at the doorway and uncovered her hair, so that people would not go into his tent to awaken him. She said, "I know that the whole community is all holy and modest and will not enter to me if my hair is uncovered." Whoever came to call him saw a woman with uncovered hair, and would go back.

Here we see what it really means to helpfully oppose. On ben Pelet's wife stood at the entrance to the tent and prevented On ben Pelet from succumbing to his weaknesses. Although he may have been initially upset by his wife's response, eventually he understood that she was saving him.

The Torah commands a man to find a woman who is, *yafeh*, which literally means "beautiful." However the Chassidic master note it is composed of the Hebrew letters *yud*, *pey*, *hey*, which are first letters of the phrase *yoshev petach ha-ohel*, "dwells at the opening of the tent." This means that a woman's real beauty is that she has the ability to stand at the entranceway of the home, so to speak, and guard the home from corruption and impurity, and only allows purity and goodness to flow through.

There is a well known contradiction in the words of King Solomon. King Solomon in Proverbs writes, "He who has found [*matza*] a wife has found goodness." However, in another place he writes, "And I have more bitter than death, the woman who snares." How are these two verses to be reconciled? The Talmud answers that many women may appear outwardly to be the same, but their actions reveal where their heart truly is. A man who finds a woman who supports her husband in the proper way, lifting him up spiritually and making him into a better more moral person, such a find is indeed finding goodness. However, a woman who erodes her husband's moral character and pulls him down to a lower place, more distant from his family and God, such a woman is in fact poison, and bitterer than death.

An Eternal Love

The Torah compares the love between man and wife with the love between God and all of Israel. It is by no coincidence that the Prophet Malachi writes, "My comrade, my wife, the source of my covenant." The word "covenant" is the same word used to describe our connection to God in the Torah. The Hebrew word *berit*, the circumcision ritual a male boy receives when he is eight days old, means "covenant" for it is the link that connects us to God. King Solomon's Song of Songs, according to many commentaries, which is on the surface a love sonnet between a man and his lover, is really about the love between God and all of Israel. God says to Israel that we are constantly beautiful to Him as it says, "Behold, you are lovely, my friend, behold you are lovely, your very appearance radiates with dovelike constancy." This is because of our deeds as it says, "You are beautiful, My love, when your deeds are pleasing, as comely now as you were in Jerusalem of old, hosts of angels stand in awe of you." A woman can keep radiating with beauty and charm when her deeds are beautiful; when she gives to others, when she is gentle, loving, and nurturing.

Moreover, according to Kabbalah, a woman is born with an extra intuition that men do not have. We find this idea beautiful illustrated in the Talmud. One of the great heroines of the Talmud is Beruriah, the wife of the great sage Rabbi Meir. There was a group of contemptible people in Rabbi Meir's neighborhood who constantly harassed Rabbi Meir with a barrage of comments. Rabbi Meir once prayed that these men should perish from this world. Beruriah overheard Rabbi Meir praying for this. She asked Rabbi Meir, "On what basis do you have to pray for this? Perhaps you will say it is because it is written in Psalms, 'And the sinners (*chata'im*) shall perish!' However, does the verse write *chotim*, "sinners"? The verse writes *chata'im*, the cause of sin, the Evil Inclination! Rather, you should pray that what causes those people to sin should perish, but not that the people themselves should perish!" Rabbi Meir took his wife's advice and prayed that the people should change their ways and indeed the people repented.

Here we see an example of where a woman was able to perceive something that her husband could not, namely the importance of separating the person from the base inclinations that sometimes cloud the person from allowing their true self to shine through. This is the special gift that women were born with, the ability to see goodness in people and situations when there husband could not.

Partners with Our Creator

The greatness of building a Jewish home is that we become partners with the Master of the World in creation. We can create a human being, the same way God created the first man and woman, and sustains the world every moment. It is for this reason that the Torah places so much emphasis on the importance of honoring one's father and mother and compares it to honoring the Almighty himself. However, if God is not allowed into the partnership, the result on the Jewish home can be quite devastating. One of the great Talmudic Sages once remarked that the Hebrew word for "man" is *ish*, which is composed of the three Hebrew letters *aleph*, *yud*, and *shin*. The Hebrew word for a "woman" is *ishah*, from the letters *aleph*, *shin*, and *hey*. The exclusive letter that a man has is *yud*, and the exclusive letter a woman has is *hey*, which together spell one of God's names. This means that it is God which comes and unites the man and woman, and He is needed to sustain the relationship. However, without these two letters, the only two remaining letters are *aleph* and *shin*, which spells *aish*, "fire." This means that without God's presence in the home, the home is in the spiritual sense destroyed. This does not mean that the couple will have an unhappy marriage, two people who are compatible and have a mutual respect and love for each other can be happy. But real Inner Happiness, happiness of two souls bonding together in complete unity, is unattainable without allowing God into the relationship as well.

An All-Encompassing Love

What is Love in the Jewish sense? Rabbi Nachman points out that the Hebrew word for Love is *ahavah*, which has the same *gematria* (numerological value) as the word *echad*, "one." For when two souls are truly united with love, they feel as if they are one. The Torah describes the uniting of a man and a woman as, "They shall become one flesh." According to one interpretation of Genesis, we find that Adam was created as one androgynous being originally, and later formed Eve from Adam. The verse writes, "And God built the side that He had taken from the man into a woman, and He brought her to the man. And the man said, 'This time it is bone of my bone and flesh of my flesh. This shall be called *ishah* ("woman") for from man (*ishah*) was she taken.'" This is why many people often describe love as *recognition* for one feels they recognize the other part of themselves that has been missing for so long. It is a feeling for many, of coming home. It is also interesting to note that the Torah describes the sexual relationship between Adam and Eve as *knowledge*. Knowledge is does not just come from studying a book, it comes from *understanding*. When someone experiences physical intimacy with the right person, he or she understands the other person completely and in turn, because this person is their missing half, they are coming to understand themselves as well.

The Love of Giving

The Hebrew word for love is *ahavah*, which comes from the root *hav*, "give." This means that when one truly gives to another person from the very essence of his being, one begins to experience Love. Indeed, many couples say that the time when they feel the strongest bond with their spouse even more that during physical intimacy is when their spouse is in a low state. During this state of state of pain or sadness, when he or she selflessly gives strength to their spouse and helps them to heal, this creates a bond that is truly unbreakable.

We see this concept in the Biblical story of Jacob and Rachel. Jacob loved Rachel dearly, but he was deceived by his own father-in-law Laban to work for fourteen years for him in order to have her hand in marriage. Interestingly enough, the verse writes that when Jacob worked for Rachel, "They seemed to him a few days because of his love for her." Ordinarily, one would think that the years would seem to drag forever! However, the commentaries explain ingeniously that it is specifically because Jacob was giving selflessly to Rachel by working for Laban, every day was a creating a stronger and stronger bond and that is why the days seemed to go by so quickly.

In this way, our relationship to our spouse is similar to our relationship with God as well. The Torah tells us that God loves us in an infinite way. We can understand this to mean that God is constantly giving to us, just as one would give to a spouse. God does not receive anything in return; He only desires that we come close to Him so we can receive His Goodness. Every commandment in the Torah is an opportunity to come close to God. And so our model for how to love one's spouse is modeled after our love for God. Furthermore, the Torah teaches us that true love comes really after an established and meaningful relationship. It says in the Torah, "Isaac married Rebecca, she became his wife, and he loved her." Here we see that first Isaac took Rebecca as his wife before he was able to experience the feelings of love for her. This is similar to one's love for God; one does not usually feel a strong love for God, one only begins to love Him after an established committed relationship to Him. After prayer, after fulfilling the Divine ordinances, after studying His word, we begin to appreciate and truly love God and His Goodness.

So it is in our relationships with the opposite sex. After years of sharing, opening up, expressing our fears and desires, building, laughing, and crying, only then does a real love begin to develop. Only then, does real trust begin, when one feels they have helped their other half fulfill their dreams, when one has opened up to their most vulnerable parts of themselves, and in turn helped their spouse discuss theirs. This is real Love, not Hollywood Love, but Torah Love, love as it was meant to be. I have always felt that true love proves the existence of a higher spiritual world, for although people may say that sex is the greatest of all physical pleasures, everyone agrees when it is done in the context of love, it is infinitely greater.

Loving Unconditionally

One final thought about the Jewish view of Love. In *Pirkei Avot* it is written, "Any love that is dependent on something will not endure, and any love that is not dependent on something will endure forever." The text goes on to give examples of these two forms of love. In the Bible, it writes of Amnon having a 'love' for Tamar, which was really based on physical infatuation. After Amnon forced himself on Tamar, it is written that he hated Tamar, with an even greater passion than his imagined 'love' for her. Yes, there is 'love' here, but the reality is the only person Amnon 'loved' is himself! He only saw her as an object of desire, of lust, and after it was gone, so was his imagined 'love' for her! So many people think Love is a list of qualities, very often starting with the physical that makes him or her love the other person. However, the reality is, love has very little to do with a 'list.' For if the 'list' is gone, so is the love. Real Love goes much deeper than that, and is just there from a deep intimate soul to soul connection that is not dependent on anything. Where do we find this? *Pirkei Avot* goes on to give the example of the love of Kind David and Jonathan. This was a real love, not based on sex at all, for both of them were men, but a love based on a real deep understanding of each other; a soul-to-soul connection.

For those of you who are currently searching for that special someone, I wanted to share one final thought with you. Many of us have heard that well known phrase from the Talmud, "Making a match is as difficult as splitting the sea." The question arises why is that difficult for God to do? For God splitting the sea is as easy as anything else for Him to do, for He created Nature and so bending Nature should be as easy as any occurrence in the natural world? The Alexander Rebbe gives a most ingenious answer. He explains that it is all a matter of perspective. If we *only* believe that matches are made by us, then in fact, it is as difficult as splitting the sea, for that is a feat that none of us can do. But if we recognize that God plays a role, then in fact it is as *easy* as splitting the sea, for He can do *anything*. When we come to realize that we alone cannot make a match because it is too difficult for us, when we recognize we need God to come down and help us, only then can we begin to finally find (and keep) the special someone in our lives. On our own, we are powerless, but with His help we are powerful beyond measure. Keeping Him in our lives after the relationship begins also helps us keep comfort, stability, and meaning in our relationships as well. So pray each day that He comes to bring you the right person into your life and for His guidance in making the right decisions.

My blessing to everyone is to find that special spouse who really brings out the best in us, who accepts us for who we are, who cares for us, in the deepest way, and who we in turn can do the same for them. And for those who have already found that special person, to be able to appreciate their goodness, and that they are, indeed, their other half.

Spiritual Exercises

1. Try to remember a time when you were feeling in love. How did you feel during that time? How did you feel toward God and life in general?

2. Jot down some of the things you feel love is. Does it coincide with the Torah's views on Love? What can you do to make the concept and experience of love more meaningful in your personal life?

3. What are some mistakes you have made with regard to Love? Try to think of some ways to improve your attitude and behavior toward Love to make it more real and meaningful.

4. Try to take a few minutes each day to think about and appreciate the people in your life that you love the most. Think about why your relationship with them is so special. If necessary, jot these thoughts down, keep them with you at all times, and take them out for a few moments each day and study them. Then chronicle how these few minutes of contemplation effect your day and your life in general.

Chapter 10
Finding the Land of Israel Inside of You

I am the Lord, the God of your father Abraham and the God of Isaac; the land on which you lie, I will give it to you and to your descendants. Your descendants shall also be like the dust of the earth, and you shall spread out to the west and to the east and to the north and to the south; and in you and in your descendants shall all the families of the earth be blessed. And behold, I am with you, and will keep you wherever you go, and will bring you back to this land; for I will not leave you until I have done what I have promised you.

~ Genesis 28

CLOSE YOUR EYES FOR A minute. Imagine you are walking with your wife and children carrying the fruit baskets in your hand, known as *Bikkurim,* to the Temple Mount. It is a clear spring day, with a warm breeze in the air. You and your family make your way to the Temple Mount, surrounded by throngs of other Jews from all over the world. As you look over the hills, you can see they are filled with Jews from all walks of life, and all ages, the pitter-patter of footsteps, the sound of children laughing, people singing, as they joyously make their way to the most sanctified place on earth.

Although some years have passed since those times, those footsteps still resonate deep within our consciousness and if one listens closely, one can still here their echo.

To the Jew, there is no place on earth quite like the Land of Israel.

Every clump of earth in the Land of Israel is rich with the history of our People. We are linked to the Land for the past four thousand years. God spoke to our forefather Abraham, "Go for yourself, from your land, from your family, and from your father's house to the land that I will show you." These were the first words He ever spoke to Abraham, the very first Jew. It is only in the Land of Israel that the Jewish People can truly prosper as God continues and says, "And I will make of you a great nation; I will bless you, and make your name great, and you shall be a blessing." Rabbi Nachman of Breslov used to say that wherever a Jew goes, he is going to the Land of Israel. This means that even if a Jew lives in a distant land, there is a part of him that always yearns to be in the Land of Israel.

Thus the Jewish People were connected to the Land long before we were given the Torah and forged into a People. Rabbi Mordechai Greenberg writes that this is what makes the Jewish People's connection to the Land of Israel unique. For most people, their connection to a country begins once they settle there, but for the Jewish People, the connection began even before they settled there.

It is written in the Torah, "Build for Me a Sanctuary and I will dwell in *them*." The grammar appears to be inappropriate. Shouldn't it say, "And I will dwell in *it*"? If the verse is speaking about God dwelling in the Sanctuary, it should say God dwells "in it"! The commentaries explain that the verse means when we enter the place where God resides, He dwells inside each and every one of us. The verse is not talking about Him; it is talking about *us*. The same concept can certainly be applied to the Land of Israel as a whole. This is the home where God resides and when we are in it, God resides in each and every one of us.

Furthermore if there is a spark of Godliness in each of us, then the Land of Israel exists in all of us. It is the home that we all strive to one day live in just as the Divine Presence longs to return.

The Miracle of the Modern State

Thankfully, we live in a time when the Land of Israel is once again in our hands. Sadly enough, many Jews disregard the miraculous birth of the modern day State of Israel as an insignificant event since it came about in a natural manner and through secular people. However, this is an inappropriate perspective. The miracle of the story of Esther teaches us that often the greatest of all miracles can come about in a natural manner. It is up to us to see the Hand of God in everything. Furthermore, the Torah proves to us that salvation can come through irreligious people. Rabbi Aron Soloveichik writes extensively about the tremendous religious significance of the birth of the State of Israel. He quotes a story from the Bible that proves that redemption can come through people that are irreligious. The story is about four lepers who were excommunicated and were forced to live outside of the Jewish camp. The leprosy we speak of here is a spiritual form of leprosy, and was the punishment in Biblical times for speaking words of *lashon hara*, damaging gossip. The story occurred during a famine, when the Jews were on the verge of total starvation. These four lepers decided to sneak into a tent of the Philistine army, which was encamped next door one night and steal some food as they too were famished. They discovered that during the night, the Philistine army fled, leaving behind all of their food! The lepers could not believe their luck. They had only discovered this since they were outside of the Jewish camp and were thus able to sneak into the Philistine camp. The lepers went back into the Jewish camp and informed the Jewish leaders that the Philistine army had fled, and the Jewish people were able to go to where the Philistines had encamped and partake of all the food they left behind. Thus the famine ended, and the saviors were none other than these four lepers, who were sinners.

So it was with the modern day State. Although many of the people who brought about the creation of the state were not religious people, and some were even anti-religious, nevertheless the spiritual benefits we have received as a people have been unparalleled in recent history. Now, for the first time in nearly two thousand years, Jews are free to go to the Land of Israel to visit, to study, to visit the holy sites, and most importantly, to *live.*

The Uniqueness of the Land of Israel

The uniqueness of the Land of Israel is that it is the only country in the world that is given the unique task of infusing the sacred into the profane, the religious into the secular. Rabbi Mordechai Greenberg writes this is what impressed the Queen of Sheba so much in the days of King Solomon. The verse writes, "The Queen of Sheba saw all the wisdom of Solomon, the palace that he had erected; ... and the *olah* [burnt-offering] that he brought to the Temple of God—and she was overwhelmed." What was so special about this *olah* that impressed her? The Malbim explains that there is actually a parallel verse elsewhere that uses the word *aliyato*, "his ramp, instead of *olah*. What impressed her was that there was a ramp or passageway leading from the Holy Temple to the Palace. What she saw was that there was a connection between the King and religion. In Judaism, everything is based on Divine inspiration and guidance; nothing is divorced from spirituality. This is why there is the Sages put so much emphasis on justice being based on Torah Law. This reiterates this principle. This is the mission that the modern day State of Israel is given.

In Kabbalah, it is written that there are four mystical cities in the Land of Israel: Jerusalem, Safed, Hebron, and Tiberias. Let us explore each of these great cities and the unique color which each one brings to our People.

The City of Jerusalem

Undoubtedly, the greatest of all of these cities is Jerusalem. Jerusalem has captured the imagination of Jewish writers for thousands of years. Rabbi Judah HaLevi, author of the *Kuzari*, dreamed of visiting the holy city, as expressed in his writings; sadly enough he never made it there. Countless other writers express the unearthly beauty and sanctity of the city. Rabbi Tzvi Yehudah Kook wrote:

> Just as in the human body, the heart is the central and essential organ, so too Jerusalem is vital to the rest of the Land of Israel. Of course Haifa, Beer Sheva belong to us, just as Tel Aviv does as well, each is one of our limbs.
>
> But to Jerusalem, there is central, essential significance; it is the inner source of our strength, of our nation-Torah, prophecy, the Temple, and Monarchy. Jerusalem is the seat of the *Sanhedrin,* the cornerstone of our nation, the valley of prophecy, the place of the Temple, the Capital of the Monarchy. It is the city that is the essence of our nationality, our

spiritual legacy, our history, our value system, where we join together as one.

The sanctity of Jerusalem does not become revealed amidst the sanctity that fills all corners of our Land, rather quite the opposite, Jerusalem pumps sanctity to all other limbs of the land of Israel; it is the essential sanctity.

To our People, the city has always been at the forefront of our minds. We say three times a day in our prayers, "And our eyes long for the return to Jerusalem." At the highest moments of the year, we temper our state of joy with mourning for the destruction of Jerusalem. At every Jewish wedding at the climax of the wedding when the bride and groom are bonded together under the *chuppah* (marriage canopy) a glass is broken by the groom and we sing, "If we forget Jerusalem let the strength of my right hand be weakened, if I fail to elevate Jerusalem over my foremost joy." Even at the end of Yom Kippur, when we are at the height of joy for our sins being absolved, we sing, "Next year in Jerusalem." And on Passover, when we celebrate freedom and commemorate the Exodus from Egypt, we end the night singing, "Next year in Jerusalem." This is because no matter where we are or how happy we feel, we realize our lives are not complete until we are back in Jerusalem and Jerusalem is completely restored to its former glory.

Jerusalem is known as the City of Gold. Kings David and Solomon rebuilt the city over three thousand years ago. There is a well known Talmudic dictum that says, "Ten measures of beauty descended into the world. Of them, Jerusalem took nine." Jerusalem, in the glory days of King Solomon when the First Temple was built, had unparalleled beauty. Moreover, this was the land where the prophets spoke God's word, where the Levites sang in service of the Lord, where the great tribunal sat, where the scholars studied and debated. When one walks through the streets of Jerusalem today, one can still hear the echoes of the voices of yesteryear. Every street corner pulsates with holiness and sanctity; every stone and hill has a story to be told. The Holy Wall still stands to this day, as promised over two thousand years ago by the Midrash that the Western Wall will never fall. Jews from all walks of life come and pour their hearts to their Father in Heaven as they embrace those precious stones. In the words of Rabbi Tzvi Yehudah Kook, "There are human hearts that are made of stone, and there are stones made of human hearts."

Rabbi David Aron once said something quite remarkable about the prayer we say every day when we ask for Jerusalem to be rebuilt. The paragraph begins with, "*And* for Jerusalem, Your City." This is the only benediction in the *Shemoneh Esreh* that begins with the word "And." Obviously there is a link between this passage and the passage that preceded it, which is about the righteous people in the world. What connection is there between Jerusalem and righteous people? Rabbi Aron explains that the same way righteous people are the gems of the Jewish People who bring down God's Word into the world, so too Jerusalem is the treasure of the world and it is the center that spreads the Word of God to the world. This is the profound connection between the righteous and Jerusalem.

As expressed earlier, we see from Kabbalah and from Song of Songs a powerful metaphor of the love of God to His People is comparable to the love of a man to his wife. The day of the wedding, so to speak, is the Sabbath, as the Sabbath is compared to a beautiful bride. It was for this reason, as will be explained later, why the Torah was given on the Sabbath. And if we are to take the metaphor one step further, the place of the wedding is the city of

Jerusalem, with the Holy Temple as the *chuppah*. This is expressed most succinctly in the prayer we say on Shavuot when we celebrate receiving the Torah. The words are, "To the City of Jerusalem as He gathers in the Exile. His Divine Presence will shelter her during days and nights, His bridal canopy to be built in her crowned with praises; with brilliant clouds to beautify the canopy." The commentaries explain this is an allegorical reference to the days when of the Messiah when the new Temple will be like a canopy for the wedding between God and Israel.

King David writes, "Jerusalem is a city that is united together." This is explained in the Talmud to mean that Jerusalem is what brings the Jewish People together, as when we made our Pilgrimage three times a year to Jerusalem in Temple times. When one walks the streets, one can envision the pitter-patter sounds of thousands of footsteps as thousands of Jews together made the Pilgrimage. To this day, Jerusalem still unites us, for it is one of the only places in the world where Jews from all walks of life gather to pray at the Western Wall.

The City of Tzfat (Safed)

The city of Tzfat is also extraordinary. The old city of Tzfat is full of legend and lore. It was here that the great Rabbi Isaac Luria (Arizal), one of the greatest Kabbalists who ever lived, walked and spread his teachings. It was said that the Arizal was visited by nearly every night by Rabbi Shimon Bar Yochai himself, the great author of the Zohar, one of the definitive works of Jewish mysticism and spirituality. The special *mikveh* (ritual bath) that the Arizal immersed in every morning still exists to this very day. His *mikveh* is a natural stream flowing from the depths of a cave. Legend has it that anyone who immersed in the Arizal's *mikveh* even once would some day truly repent from all of his or her sins and return to God wholeheartedly. It was in this great city that many of the great Kabbalists lived and where Kabbalah flourished. It was here that *Kabbalat Shabbat*, the prayer that is said to welcome in the Sabbath on Friday night, was first formulated. And it was here that one of the great Kabbalists, Rabbi Shlomo HaLevi Alkabetz composed the beautiful and inspiring song *Lechah Dodi* ("Come My Beloved, to Meet the Bride, Let Us Welcome the Sabbath"), which is the song we sing to this very day to usher in the Sabbath. It was said that the great Kabbalists used to greet the Sabbath in the woods in order to be in touch with nature on the Holy Day. Nearly every ancient synagogue in the Old City of Tzfat has a story to tell. Each synagogue is replete with legends of miracles and mystical experiences.

The City of Tiveriah (Tiberias)

Tiveriah is another of the ancient cities mentioned in Kabbalah, famous for its nourishing and natural hot springs. It is built in the north of Israel, alongside the beautiful Kinneret River. It is here that the Talmud declares that Moses' sister Miriam's well bubbled up from the depths of its lake, the Sea of Galilee. Miriam's well was mentioned in the Bible and was said to be one of God's last creations as the sun set on the world's first Sabbath. From here it was magically transported to the desert of Sinai for the children of Israel to have water when they wandered there. The Talmud writes that Tiveriah comes from the word *tibbor*, "navel," because it is the center of the Land of Israel and the perhaps it was because it was the center of Torah study in the time of the Talmud. For over three centuries, the Oral Law was expounded there and the *Sanhedrin* (Jewish Tribunal) was housed there. It is believed that Rabbi Judah the Prince completed compiling the Mishnah there,

169

and it was here that the Jerusalem Talmud was written. Centuries later, the great Kabbalist Rabbi Moshe Chaim Luzzatto, author of *Mesillat Yesharim* (Path of the Just) and *Derech Hashem* (The Way of God) lived much of his life there. He is buried in his beloved city at the feet of his mentor, the Talmudic Sage Rabbi Akiva. It is written that the Redemption of Israel would commence from the city of Tiberius. Moreover, Maimonides mentioned a tradition that the *Sanhedrin* would first convene in Tiberius before moving to the rebuilt Temple in Jerusalem.

The City of Chevron (Hebron)

Finally, there is the ancient Biblical city of Chevron. It was here that the Talmud writes is one of the places that Jews can always claim rights to, as the Bible records our forefather Abraham bought the piece of Land from Ephron for 400 silver coins as a burial place for his wife Sarah. Nearly all of the Patriarchs and Matriarchs are buried in Hebron, in *Ma'arat HaMachpelah* (The Tomb of the Patriarchs). The Zohar writes that this spot is the entranceway to the Garden of Eden. This site is visited by thousands of Jews throughout the year till this very day. It remains a place of solace and comfort, as well as a place to beseech our great Patriarchs and Matriarchs to pray to God for mercy on their behalf. The name *Chevron* is derived from the Hebrew word *chibbur*, "connection," because the city of Chevron serves as a connection between Heaven and Earth. The burial site of the Patriarchs and Matriarchs is perhaps the greatest connection we have to Heaven. It connects us to our past as well as to our future. It is said in Jewish Tradition that at the end of time the Resurrection of the Dead will begin in the city of Chevron.

There is an incredible story about how the Jewish presence returned to Chevron. For many years, the ancient

Jewish cemetery in Chevron remained closed, as it was feared there would be an Arab reprisal if the cemetery was re-opened. Until one young woman named Sarah who lived in Chevron had a baby boy. She named Abraham, after our holy father Abraham. Sadly enough, the baby died shortly after he was born. Late one night, the young woman took her baby and a shovel to the Jewish cemetery. Many of the guards surrounding the cemetery tried to stop her, but she remained adamant and continued on her trek. Many of the guards followed her as well as some other people passing by. Soon a small crowd followed her into the cemetery. She knelt down on the floor beside an open spot and began to weep. This is what she said, "Over three thousand years ago, our holy father Abraham knelt down on this very earth to bury his beloved wife Sarah. Now, I, Sarah am returning to bury my son Abraham right here on this very same earth." There was total silence as she began to dig. One by one, the people began to dig with her. This one woman's bravery began the rebirth of the ancient cemetery and helped foster the Jewish presence in Chevron.

To me, this story, above all, captures the essence of our People in recent history. It is written in the verse, "And Your children shall return to their borders." This means that we will return once again to the Land of Israel and relive what our ancestors once did, beginning with our Father Abraham and continuing till the present day.

This is just a glimpse into the four mystical cities mentioned in the Kabbalah. To truly experience these cities, one must visit them, walk on their sacred ground, and marvel at their mysteries.

The Land in Our Hearts

For the Jew, the Land of Israel is always in our hearts and minds. Rabbi Shlomo Carlebach used to bless people in the following way, "When a Jew walks away from the *Kotel* (Western Wall), he does not simply turn around and walk away, he walks away backwards. When a person meets with the Czar of Russia, he does not turn around and walk away, but rather he walks away backwards. I bless you that your whole life we should walk away backwards. Keep your eyes on the *Kotel* and Jerusalem, wherever you are. Keep your eyes on the Land of Israel."

I end this chapter with one of my favorite Torah ideas that I heard from my Rebbe, Rav Moshe Weinberger. This idea will explain why I named this chapter "Finding the Land of Israel Inside of You." The Talmud discusses various Talmudic Sages who demonstrated their love for the Land of Israel. One sage used to kiss the stones by the city of Acco, for there was the entranceway into the land of Israel. Another sage used to fix the roads and alleys in Israel. And Rabbi Chiya bar Gamda used to roll around in the dirt of Israel, for it is written in the verse, "Your servants have loved her stones and cherished her dirt." Rashi comments on this last opinion: He rolled around in the dirt because Your servants have loved her stones and cherished her dirt.

On the surface, this comment does not seem to be adding anything at all. Several of the commentators say, in fact, it is a printing mistake, for Rashi would not just repeat what the Talmud says. However, Rabbi Yechiel Yaakov Weinberg, known as the *Seridei Aish*, elucidates this Rashi with an extraordinary insight. Rashi repeats the passage in the Talmud, but he leaves out one crucial point: he leaves out *for it is written in the verse.* What does this mean? It means that he didn't roll in the dirt because of the verse, but because *he felt it inside of himself* the love for the Land of Israel. The verse was only secondary, a by-product of how he felt within him.

Rabbi Moshe Weinberger elaborates further: Imagine a

couple that is dating, and the moment comes when the time feels right for proposal. It is a beautiful peaceful summer night. A soft melody drifts through the air from a pool party not too far away. They walk alone together through a park, stopping every so often to gaze at the assortment of roses decorating the walkway. The air is crisp and smells of freshly cut grass and lilac. After walking in silence, he turns to her. The pounding of her heart is almost audible as she can feel the moment she has waited for so long is about to come. He whispers her name in her ear and says, "The Torah writes 'A man is supposed to take a woman as a wife.' So tonight I would like to ask you to marry me to fulfill the Torah commandment."

What a letdown! Making a proposal because the Torah commanded it! Is this what love is all about? What about the feelings inside of a person telling him that he is right for her? What about the deep soulful connection that two people feel who know that the other person completes their destiny? Real love isn't based on someone being told to love someone, or because it is written somewhere to have love for someone or somewhere!

This is the potent lesson that Rashi was teaching us. This great sage didn't express his feelings for the Land of Israel because it was written in the verses. It is because he knew and felt it deep within himself. May we all experience this deep and inner love for the Land of our Forefathers, the Land of our People, the Land of our souls.

Spiritual Exercises

1. Try to think of a time when you felt totally connected to the Land of Israel, either from a trip to Israel or an event about Israel, or even a movie about Israel. What made it feel special to you? Why do you feel that event or moment you connected with Israel so much?

2. Try to think of your reaction when hearing news about events going on in the Land of Israel, either happy or tragic events. How did you feel at the time? What made you feel that way?

3. Try to close your eyes for a few moments each day and think about the Land and People of Israel. Try to think of a city or place that you feel most connected to.

4. Try to make a point to learn more about the history of Israel, from biblical times to the present day. Try to learn some Torah ideas that connect you to the Land of Israel.

5. Try to make it a point to visit Israel at least once a year, for as long as possible. While there, try to visit places that connect you to the spiritual character of the Land. If possible, start to think of options for moving there one day as well.

Chapter 11
The Beauty of Torah

When He made the world, He decided He would take
the role of Kindness. That way, when we would be kind,
we could bond to Him with our kindness. He decided to
have Wisdom. That way, by being wise, we could bond
to Him and His wisdom. He decided to be conscious of
Himself, so that we could attain consciousness of that
which is beyond knowing. And all this He gave to us in
His Torah. He gave us Himself.

~ Rabbi Menachem Mendel Schneerson

THE STORY IS TOLD ABOUT the *Tzemach Tzedek*, the third Lubavitcher Rebbe, the grandson of the Rabbi Shneur Zalman of Liadi, author of the *Tanya*. When the Tzemach Tzedek was only nine or ten years old, he wanted so badly to hear a *shi'ur* (Torah lecture) from his grandfather, R. Shneur Zalman. The problem was that the *shi'ur* was only open to the elite Chassidim and took place in R. Shneur Zalman's private study. So what did the Tzemach Tzedek do? Right outside of the private study was on old furnace that was turned off. The Tzemach Tzedek crawled inside of the furnace and pressed his ear against the wall. When he did this, he was able to hear the entire lecture. This went on for quite some time until one day someone in the house was cold and went to turn on the furnace. Right after turning it on, he right away heard screaming and coughing coming from the inside. Horrified, the person reached inside and pulled out the young boy. Miraculously, the boy had not been hurt yet. By this time, the lecture had stopped and R. Shneur Zalman ran outside to see what was going on. He saw the little boy covered in soot and ashes, coughing and thrashing.

Smiling, R. Shneur Zalman reached down and stroked the little boy's child. "It is a privilege and an honor to have you as a grandchild. Tonight you have reached a level much higher than anyone who attended my *shi'ur*. For the Torah was given through fire, and you who was willing to go through fire to hear words of Torah will reach heights one day that are unimaginable. What a scholar you will be one day."

This boy, of course, grew up to be the great Tzemach Tzedek, the third Lubavitcher Rebbe.

The story illustrates the internal fire the that the truly righteous possess that motivates them to study words of Torah. The question, of course, is: How do we get to that place? How do we get a little taste of what the Tzemach Tzedek already had as a young boy? What can we do, in our own small way, to hear the echo of Mount Sinai?

God Is Speaking to Us

The answer lies in our perception of what the Torah is, and in what it can do for us. I heard an incredible idea from a rabbi I was close to in Baltimore that has made a huge impact on how I perceive what the Torah is. The lecture took place before Hanukkah, and the rabbi was explaining how the wisdom of the Torah is different than any other wisdom, especially Greek wisdom. After all, we all know that there is incredible wisdom in chemistry, physics, mathematics, and biology. What is unique about Torah wisdom?

He answered this question with another question. It says in *Pirkei Avot* that if someone is studying the Torah and sees a beautiful tree or field and interrupts his studies to comment, "What a beautiful tree that is!" he is regarded as if he bears guilt for his soul. The question is: What is so bad about what this person did? Isn't it also a way to connect to God through appreciating nature? Why does the Torah regard him as "if he bears guilt for his soul" which is a phrase usually reserved for something very wrong?

The rabbi answered this question with a parable. Imagine a person reading the most incredible book he has ever read. Every word seems rich and laden with meaning, the characters have depth and the storyline is riveting. He cannot seem to turn the pages fast enough. In the middle of while he is reading the book, he gets a tap on the shoulder and standing over there is the author of the book himself. The author tells him he wants to tell him about his book. Incredibly, the reader asks to just be left alone, he just wants to read his book! Such a person is essentially a fool, because here is the opportunity to glean all of the insight and inspiration that went into the book, all of the deeper meanings, and symbolism behind the written word. If the book is incredible, how much more speaking to the author himself!

This is the parable about our Torah. The entire world is, so to speak, God's book. It is his masterpiece, his *magnum opus,* as it were, and each one of God's beautiful creations is a powerful testimony to His Greatness. But when we study Torah, this is an opportunity to speak to the Author Himself. God speaks to us through the words of His prophets and the Sages. God tells us how to lead a Godly life. As Rabbi Yisrael Salanter once said, "When we pray, we go up and speak to God. But when we learn Torah, God comes down and speaks to *us*."

The Ability to Transform

This is why the Torah has the ability to change people. No other subject in the world has this ability. One can study biology, astronomy, physics, and still be an immoral person. However, this is not the case when it comes to Torah. People who study it often are changed by the experience. All over the world, in communities where Torah is studied frequently, there are less incidents of crime and moral values remain strong and steady. In Deuteronomy it says, "May my utterance flow like the dew; like storm winds upon vegetation and like raindrops upon grass." Rashi explains that just as rain strengthens the grass and makes them grow, words of Torah strengthen those who learn them and make them grow.

This is also, the mystics explain, why the law is that the Torah must be written on animal hide, and the letters first etched into the parchment before they are filled in with ink. The animal hide represents the animalistic tendencies that Man has. However, the Torah has the ability to make an *etch* into the animal hide, figuratively meaning it has the ability to make an engraving into this animal side in us and fill it with purity. Torah has the ability to transform Man.

There is a beautiful *Midrash* which illustrates this point. A king once called over his trusted servants and told them about a river with great healing powers. He gave his servants buckets, barrels, and a truck and asked his servants to load a truck with these waters. The king left the scene, and the servants began to fill the buckets with the water from the river. The problem was, the servants soon discovered, the buckets had holes in them! By the time the servants reached the truck, much of the water leaked out of the buckets and onto the ground. Frustrated, all of the servants gave up, believing the king had made some sort of mistake. Only one servant fully believed in the king, and continued tirelessly to fill the truck with as much water as he could. By the end of the day, there was some water in the barrels in the truck, but not much. When the king returned, he was disappointed in all of the servants, except for the one who put his faith completely in the king. The king explained, "My purpose in asking this from all of you was not only to fill the truck with the water, but also to clean the buckets. With each trip, the buckets would become a little cleaner."

So it is with the Torah. Much of one's Torah that one learns throughout one's lifetime becomes lost, especially without consistent review. However, much like in the parable, the healing waters of Torah that passes through the bucket that is our mind and soul has the ability to cleanse us and purify us, even if much of it escapes through the cracks.

This of course does not mean the Torah alone is foolproof. A person has to be receptive and *want* to change in order for the Torah to take an effect. And there will always be struggles, as we see still exist even within the world of Torah. For we are all still human, and no one is completely above his or her base desires. But the Torah has the ability to give us guidance and direction. It has the ability to open channels within us and create a longing for Godliness.

We see this most acutely in the story of Rabbi Akiva. As mentioned before, Rabbi Akiva came from the most humble beginnings. He was a shepherd, an unrespectable profession. He had a hatred for Torah scholars, to the point where he once declared if he saw a Torah scholar, he would want to run over to him and bite him like a donkey. And then, at the age of forty, Rabbi Akiva witnessed a small phenomenon in nature that would change his life forever. He saw a stream with a little waterfall that poured onto a rock. After splashing on the rock over a great deal of time, the water had penetrated a hole through the rock. Rabbi Akiva observed this and said, "If water can eventually pierce through something as hard as a rock, perhaps the words of Torah, which is compared to water, can pierce through the rock which is my heart."

Perhaps, the one place where we see how the Torah had changed Rabbi Akiva so fundamentally is in the following exposition. Throughout the Torah, many words are introduced by the word *et*. Although this word has no meaning by itself, the Talmudic Sages were able to expound on each of these and find deeper meanings to each of them within the context of the scriptural passage. However, there was one use of *et* that mystified all of the Sages: *Et Hashem Elokecha Tira*, "The Lord your God, you shall fear." What could the *et* in this verse possibly come to include? Rabbi Akiva came and explained that it was to include Torah Scholars, that one should fear Torah Scholars as one would fear God, for they are the ones who transmit His Word. What a radical difference from the young Akiva, the shepherd boy who hated Torah Scholars to the point where he would want to bite them as a donkey would! Here we see how deeply the Torah can affect a person; how the words can penetrate a person so his very nature can change. The angry ignorant shepherd boy no longer existed; the saintly and wise Sage, Rabbi Akiva, replaced him.

Another example where we see how deeply the Torah can change a person is in the Talmudic story of Reish Lakish. Resh Lakish was a thief, a petty criminal who belonged to a gang that thrived on stealing from the wealthy. Once he saw a beautiful woman standing on the other side of a river. In his zealousness to meet her, he leapt across the river. Little did he know that this was the daughter of the great Talmudic Sage Rabbi Yochanan. Rabbi Yochanan observed this feat and remarked, "How zealous is this young man, if only he would channel his energies into something meaningful!" Rabbi Yochanan made the following proposal to Reish Lakish: "I will allow you to marry my daughter on the condition that you allow me to take you as a disciple to study Torah." Reish Lakish agreed. From that moment on Reish Lakish became a disciple of Rabbi Yochanan. Reish Lakish's wisdom in Torah knowledge grew so great, that he would challenge his teacher in *halachic* rulings and often his opinion became the accepted one. When Reish Lakish passed away, Rabbi Yochanan mourned the loss of his prized pupil, and was consumed with an extreme sadness.

One place where we see how deeply the Torah had changed Reish Lakish was in the area of money. Normally, the Torah requires two witnesses for every loan transaction. However, the Talmud says that Reish Lakish was an exception, since he *was so trustworthy when it came to money* that even one witness would suffice. Incredible! This was the same Reish Lakish who had once been a thief, someone who thrived on taking money from others! What had changed? Reish Lakish had changed, for the Torah had changed him.

The Torah itself alludes to the ability is has to change someone. It is written regarding the cherubim, the two forms of an angel whose wings touched one another "*beaten* shall you make them." The *cherubim* rested on the top of the Ark of the Covenant, which represented the Torah, as they contained the original Tablets that Moses held before they were broken by the sin of the Golden Calf. Rashi explains that the word beaten comes to signify that the cherubim had to be formed out of the gold lid on top of the Ark, and not just built later onto the lid. Why was this so necessary? Perhaps to signify that the Torah is what *forms* a person; it can mold us into angels much as the cherubim were. The Torah is not something external to the person, but rather it is very much who we are. The wings of the cherubim pointed heavenward, just as the Torah gives us the ability to reach the Heavens.

Making Torah a Part of Us

However, in order for the Torah to penetrate our hearts, we have to make the Torah a part of who he us. The Kotzker Rebbe once said that according to Jewish Law if one were to stand under the wedding canopy and say to his bride "Behold you are betrothed to me," it doesn't mean anything until he recites the words "*to me*." It is the same idea with Torah. One can study it and meditate upon its words, but if one doesn't make it personal, if someone doesn't personalize his or her Torah and make it a part of who they are, then it doesn't mean anything. One has to want to make the Torah real to them. The Torah is called a "Tree of Life for all those who grasp it." This means that one cannot look at the Torah from afar as an abstract, dry intellectual subject, one has to truly want to *grasp* it, to bring it closer to them, and only then can it become a Tree of Life.

A Book of Love

Another way to experience the Torah as something special is to remember the one true reason why it was given to us. God gave us the Torah not because He wanted to be glorified through it. This is a common misconception that many people have, which leads one to believe that God gave it to us for His benefit. Rather, God gave us the Torah because He loves us. This is a Love that is Infinite, the *Midrash* says:

What is the meaning of the verse, "Whatever the Lord wills, he has done in Heaven and on Earth"? This may be compared to a king who decreed, "The Romans may not go to Syria and the Syrians may not go to Rome." Later on, the king desired to marry a Syrian woman, so he abolished the decree, saying, "From now on, Romans may go to Syria and Syrians may go up to Rome, and I shall begin!"

So when the Holy One created His world, He said, "The Heavens are for the Lord and the Earth he has given to the sons of Man." When he desired to give the Torah to His people Israel, He said, "From now on, those above may go up to those below, and those above may go down to those below, and I will go down first!" As it says, "The Lord descended onto Mount Sinai," and afterward, "And onto Moses, He said 'Go up onto the Lord.'" Verily, "Whatever the Lord wills, He has done on Heaven and on Earth!"

This is a powerful Midrash indeed. For in it we see the true purpose of the giving of the Torah. The Torah was not given to subjugate us to an oppressive Ruler, but to bring us closer to Him. This means that God so to speak built a Bridge linking Heaven and Earth, and the Torah is that bridge. Thus the Torah, was given out of love, and serves as our connection to the Divine. This is perhaps why the Torah was given on the Sabbath, as the Talmud teaches us. The Sabbath, as we know from the Friday night prayer service is compared to a Bride, and we are her Groom. Thus the Torah is the bond created between God and His People, similar to the bond created between man and his wife.

We see this concept also in a teaching in the Talmud. The verse writes, "Moses commanded to us the Torah, it is a *morashah* [inheritance] for the congregation of Jacob."

However, the Jerusalem Talmud explains that the word *morashah* should be read *me'urasah*, "betrothed." Thus the Torah was *betrothed* to the Jewish People. In a betrothal there is a marriage contract written between a man and his wife. The Torah serves as the contract for the betrothal between God and His People.

The holiday of Simchat Torah is the day of completion of the Torah and it is a day of celebration and dancing. A story is told that during the Holocaust, one day, a small group of beaten, forlorn Jews realized through counting days that that day was Simchat Torah. Incredibly, despite the painful situation they were all in, they decided that as Jews they needed to dance. However, they wondered, how could they dance, if they did not have a Torah to dance with? A nine-year-old boy spoke up. "I will be your Torah Scroll," he declared. And so they picked up the little boy and danced with him as one would with a Torah. The message of the story is very powerful; namely that each of us has the ability to become a living Torah, as this nine-year-old boy did. It is for this reason that Jewish Law obligates us to accord the same honor to a Torah Scholar as we would to a Torah Scroll itself. One who studies the words and truly absorbs them becomes just as great as the words themselves.

Furthermore, the Torah is what gives the Jewish People meaning in life. Without it, one feels desolate and empty. I have seen in my personal life that when I started to incorporate Torah study into my daily life through *amud yomi*, studying half a page of Talmud each day, my entire day started feeling more balanced and purposeful. Sadly enough, many people don't know of the happiness that Torah can bring. A recent survey has shown that, surprisingly, many of the most successful and wealthy people are the most depressed. People who seem to have everything are often the most miserable. Today's magazines are replete with stories of wealthy actors and actresses with dysfunctional lives, many of which resort to alcohol or drugs in an attempt to find happiness. Why is this so? Perhaps this is because they have been denying a part of themselves for so long, namely the Godly part in them that yearns for more meaning.

Viktor Frankl, in his book *Man's Search for Meaning*, writes that at the core of each and every one of us is the desire to find meaning in our lives. He writes a story about a rabbi who was with him in the concentration camps who had memorized an entire tractate of Talmud. While in the camp, he would spend his time teaching the Tractate to a boy who was in the camps. This rabbi had a special glimmer is in his eye, and a soft smile that remained with him, despite the madness and suffering he was surrounded with. However, sadly enough, right when he finished teaching the young boy the Tractate, he became one of the "walking dead," all of the life in him suddenly seemed to have disappeared. He trudged with the others in the camp, with no joy but only sadness, no longer caring if he was among the living or among the dead. What had left him was his sense of meaning, and with it, went his will to live.

This is what the Torah can do for us, it is the oasis in the desert, and it is the lifeboat, which pulls us out of the abyss. The most important aspect of studying Torah is not that it is our obligation to do so, and not the broad intellectual appeal it has, but what it does to us as people. Without it, life is empty.

Something There for Everyone

In the Book of Deuteronomy it is written, "You who are standing here today, all of you, before the Lord your God. Your heads, your tribes, your elders, your officers… your small children, your women… from the hewer of you wood, till the drawer of your water, for you to pass into the covenant of the Lord your God…" The juxtapositions in these verses is startling; right after mentioning our leaders the verse goes on to mention even people who might be considered lower class workers, such as those who draw water are also included in those who stood before God that day." The emphasis is that we *all* have a portion in the Torah, we *all* can gain insight and inspiration from its wisdom.

The great thing about Torah is that there is something there for everyone. For the intellectual, the Talmud is a vast sea full of mystery, a fascinating puzzle waiting to unfold. For the practical, rationalist mind, the world of *halachah*, Jewish Law, is the most appealing. For the mystic, there are the secrets of the Kabbalah and Chassidic realm. For the poet and the linguist, there are the poetic writings of Kings David and Solomon in the Book of Psalms, the Song of Songs, and Ecclesiastes. This is what gives Torah such a broad, almost universal appeal. It is for this reason that the Torah says, "It is not in Heaven (for you) to say, 'Who can ascend to the Heaven for us and take it for us, so that we can listen to it and perform it?' Nor is it across the sea, (for you) to say, 'Who can cross to the other side of the sea for us and take it for us, so that we can listen to it and perform it?' Rather, the matter is very near to you—in your mouth and your heart—to perform it." This means that there are parts to the Torah that are accessible to everyone; nothing is too distant or lofty, but rather it remains within ones grasp. One must only seek out the part that he or she connects to the most.

Renewing Us Each Day

In the Torah it says regarding the story of the Sinai Revelation, "For all of you who stood here today." This verse is written in the present form. Rashi explains that we are to view each day as if he or she was receiving the Torah that day, meaning with the same freshness and passion as the day of the Sinai Revelation. The Alexander Rebbe says even further. He explains this to mean that when each of us experiences a moment when we see the profound beauty that is contained in the Torah, at that moment we are re-experiencing the Sinai Revelation. God has come down once again and given us the Torah anew.

Furthermore, we recite every morning the blessing thanking God for *giving* us the Torah. "Giving" is written in the present form to illustrate this point that the Torah is constantly being given each day. Each day there are ways we can learn and feel reconnected to a historic event that is still affecting us today.

There is another beautiful example of this found in the Torah. When God gave us the Torah, a voice descended from Heaven that was *ein sof,* "without end." Rashi gives two explanations of this. One interpretation is that God's voice at Sinai really never ended, in the sense that we are still connected to His Torah today and each day is a chance to renew ourselves and our passion to study it. Something new can indeed be found in it each and every day. This means God is indeed still speaking to us through the Torah today. Another explanation Rashi gives is that the word *sof* comes from *hosif,* "add." God is in reality telling us that the Torah is not meant to be added or changed in any way.

One commentator explains that these two explanations of Rashi really are intertwined. The events which occurred at Mount Sinai over 3000 years ago really were a onetime occurrence in history. However, every day we are still feeling its experience when we fulfill His word. This can be likened to a bride and groom standing under the *chuppah* (marriage canopy). The wedding was a one-time event in the history of their relationship. The marriage contract is only given once in the couples' lives, on the wedding day. However, every day the couple still feels the bond, the connection that the wedding day brought to them. The wedding has everlasting ramifications. When we stood under the great *chuppah* of Mount Sinai, God gave us His marriage contract, His written and oral Word. Indeed, a one-time event that still continues to guide us.

May we all be privileged to see the depth and inspiration contained in the Torah, and once again re-experience the Sinai Revelation.

Spiritual Exercises

1. Try to think of a Torah passage that totally inspired you. What aspect of it did you feel you connected with?

2. Try to think of an inspiring speaker in Torah who you feel totally speaks to you. What is it about them that you feel you connect with? Try to make it a point to listen to a lecture or class from them as often as you can, even if it is only for a few minutes.

3. Try to set aside a few minutes each day for Torah study, and longer, if the time is available. Monitor how this time changes your life, and how you feel about yourself each day.

4. Think of someone you know you would enjoy studying Torah with. Try to reach out to the person and begin a partnership in Torah, for the best way to study has always been with a partner.

Chapter 12
The Gift of the Sabbath

The Sabbath comes like a caress, wiping away fear, sorrow, and somber memories. It is already night when joy begins, when a beautifying surplus of soul visits our mortal bones and lingers on.

~ Abraham Joshua Heschel

A DESTITUTE PEDDLER WOULD TRUDGE from town to town selling meager wares. Once on his travels, the sky darkened as a fierce storm approached. Desperately, he tried to seek shelter, as the storm erupted and soon the ground beneath him was blanketed with snow. The wind was biting and seared through his thin overcoat till it reached his very bones. He trudged on helplessly, as the icy cold overtook him and he felt his body grow numb. Suddenly, he saw in the distance a shimmering light. He gained a second wind, hoping to find someone who can direct him where to go. He continued on to the light, until he reached an inn. Here he found warmth in front of a cozy fireplace and a comfortable bad to spend the night. A friendly gentle innkeeper directed him where to find the next town. He thanked the innkeeper and continued on, with renewed strength and vitality.

This simple, yet beautiful Chassidic parable is the story of our lives. All week long, we are trudging through the forest, until we find solace, warmth, and direction at the great inn of the Sabbath. Here we meet the innkeeper, our Father and Friend, who gives us added strength and direction to help us go on till the next week. This is what it means to live for the Sabbath, for it is the comfort and warmth in a world wrought with confusion and difficulties. Abraham Joshua Heschel, in his inimitable fashion writes of the Sabbath, "It is one of life's highest rewards, a source of strength and inspiration to endure tribulation, to live nobly. The work on weekdays and the rest on the seventh day are correlated. The Sabbath is the inspirer, the other days the inspired."

It is interesting to note that in the *Kiddush* we say on Friday night, when we sanctify the Sabbath, we say, "As a remembrance of the Exodus from Egypt." Why suddenly mentioned there? What connection can there possibly be between the Exodus from Egypt and the Sabbath? Perhaps the answer can be this very same idea. During the work week, we are very much slaves not much different than how we were once slaves in Egypt. Only here we are slaves to our bosses, our deadlines, our meetings, and our office work. We are beholden to cell phones, computers, cars, televisions, and a great many other things that dictatorially demand our attention. But on the Sabbath, we become free. We leave the servitude of the six days of the week. We once again forge our bond with our Creator just like we did during the Exodus over three thousand years ago.

As a people, we leave in the world of experience. The law of the Sabbath, among other things, is meant to create a mood. We not only shed the clothes of the work week on the Sabbath, we shed the mentality, the mood. We are not the same people on the blessed seventh day. The Sabbath is not meant to merely be a day of rest. It is that, but much more as well. The work week is a state of *becoming*; the Sabbath is a state of *being*.

The Sabbath Experience

How does one describe the bliss of the Sabbath? It cannot be described, it can only be experienced. I once heard a beautiful parable from a rabbi when he was confronted with this question. This is the parable:

A king was once driven from his royal palace during an attempted *coup d'état*. The king was forced to flee, and was literally running for his life. When he saw some of the assassins coming from a distance, he quickly ran into a nearby barn. Once inside, he ran up to the top of the barn and hid in one of the haystacks. The assassins, suspecting that the king may have gone into the barn, entered the barn. One of the men began sticking his bayonet into each of the haystacks, one by one. The king's heart pounded as he heard the footsteps getting closer and closer to the haystack that he was hiding in. In a minute, the man's footsteps stopped, and the king sensed he was right in front of the haystack he was in. For the first time in his life, the king was absolutely terrified. The man stuck his bayonet into the haystack. Lo and behold, a miracle occurred! The bayonet went right up to his nose, but no farther! The man continued sticking his bayonet into the other haystacks, thinking he stuck the bayonet far enough into the haystack where the king was. The king was overjoyed at his good fortune. Eventually the men left the barn, thinking they had been thorough enough.

Time went by, and the rebels themselves were overthrown, and the king was restored to his throne. Word got out throughout the kingdom about the miraculous incident that took place in the barn. Once, the king was traveling and stopped in a nearby inn. The innkeeper felt honored to have the king in his presence, and insisted that the king stay free of charge. However, he had one question. "What was it like up in the barn? What was it like to be literally inches away from death?"

The king was fuming that such a question could even be asked. "How dare you even ask the king such a personal question? Do you have any idea how painful and frightening that was? Why do you remind me of such things?" In a rage the king ordered that the innkeeper be killed on the spot. The king's soldiers pointed their rifle at the innkeeper as the king began to count down from ten.

"Ten, nine, eight, seven!"

The poor innkeeper got down on his knees and began pleading for his life. "Please Your Majesty, I didn't mean any harm by the question! Please spare me!"

"Six, five, four, three!"

Beads of sweat were forming on the innkeeper. "Please, please, I'm begging you, I have a wife and children…." His voice was shaking.

"Two, one!" The innkeeper's eyes closed as he gasped for one last breath.

The king stopped. He did not count down to zero. Instead, he bent down to speak into the trembling innkeeper's ear. "Do you want to know how it felt to be in that haystack inches away from death? That is *exactly* how it felt."

There is a lot of profound meaning in this parable. Some things in life one cannot just *tell* another person what something is like, the person can only appreciate it if the person himself or herself *experiences* it. Talking about what it feels like to stand at the top of the Grand Canyon or at the *Kotel* (the Western Wall). One can only appreciate it if one experiences it personally.

So it is with the Sabbath. If one examines the laws of the Sabbath from a distance, the day seems rather oppressive. So many laws with so many minute details and so many restrictions! Who can stand a day where one must be cognizant of virtually every action so as not to desecrate the Sabbath? And where did these rules come from anyways? Who imposed them on us?

All of this changes when one experiences first-hand what the Sabbath is. A person is not the same person on the Sabbath as one is during the week. The Sabbath can be a powerful emotional experience. It is perhaps for the reason that the Sabbath is compared to a Bride and a Queen, since women, who are more nurturing by nature and are more in touch with their emotional side, yearn for connection. Rabbi Joseph B. Soloveitchik writes about what his mother taught him as a young boy:

> Most of all I learned that Judaism expresses itself not only in formal compliance with the law but also in a living experience. She taught me that there is a flavor, a scent, and a warmth to the *Mitzvot.* I learned from her the most important thing in life—to feel the presence of the Almighty and the gentle pressure of His hand resting upon my frail shoulders. Without her teachings, which were often transmitted to me in silence, I would have grown up a soulless being, dry and insensitive.
>
> The laws of Shabbat, for instance, were passed on to me by my father, they are part of the *mussar avikha* (the self improvement of the father.) The Sabbath as a living entity, as a queen, was revealed to me by my mother; it is part of the *torat imekha* (the teachings of the mother). The fathers *knew* much about the Shabbat; the mothers *lived* the Shabbat, experienced her presence, and perceived her beauty and splendor.
>
> The fathers taught generations how to observe the Shabbat; mothers taught generations how to greet the Shabbat and how to enjoy her twenty-four hour presence.

Blending the Physical and Spiritual

On the Sabbath we have two loaves of bread at each of the meals. This is symbolic of the double portion of manna that we received on the eve of the Sabbath in biblical times. The manna was a very unique food; it fell directly from Heaven, could taste like any food the recipient wanted it to taste like, and did not produce any excrement. Thus the manna served as a fusion of the body and soul; it provided nourishment for the body and came from a heavenly source. This is what the Sabbath is all about; taking the mundane and elevating into something sacred. Everything we do on the Sabbath; the lavish meals and the *mitzvah* to conjugate with one's spouse is all for the purpose of arriving at a higher state of joy in order to serve God. This is what makes the Sabbath so unique.

We find the Sabbath link between the physical and spiritual most acutely at the *havdalah* ceremony. *Havdalah* is the ceremony that marks the end of the Sabbath. The three items we use in the ceremony are *besamim* (spices), wine, and of course the candle itself. What is unique about these three items?

The answer lies in looking at their unique properties. Wine, as mentioned in an earlier chapter, has both physical and spiritual elements. It provides our body with physical pleasure, yet it is used in many of our holiday services to elevate our spiritual state. It is best preserved in a simple vessel; much like the Torah is preserved best in a person who is humble. Smelling spices also has physical and spiritual elements; as scent is a pleasure we enjoy even though it does not provide us with any physical nourishment. Finally we examine the *havdalah* candle; which too is rooted in the physical, but soars to the spiritual. The candle is made from wax and thread, yet the flame is intangible, it is constantly changing, it provides light, warmth, beauty, and inspiration.

This is why we depart the Sabbath with these three items in our hand; the Sabbath the eternal bridge between our world and the next must exit with objects that serve as the conduit between the body and the soul.

Day of Rest, Day of Eternity

Perhaps it is for this reason that the Sabbath occurs on the seventh day. The number six represents the physical world, as we know it was created in six days. (Whether the Torah was literal in its depiction of the six days of creation or figurative is a discussion beyond the scope of this book.) Furthermore, the six days represent the work week, as it is written, "for six days you shall work." The number eight represents eternity, that which is beyond this world. A Jewish baby boy is circumcised on the eight day, signifying his link to the Eternal People. We wear garments called *tzitzit*, which have eight strings on each corner, representing a spiritual garment to clothe our physical bodies. But what does the number seven represent? Seven is the link, the bridge between six and eight, between temporality and eternity.

It also can be part of the reason why in the *Kiddush* on the Sabbath we mention the exodus from Egypt. Egypt represents physicality, and slavery, not much different from the slavery we experience daily during our week of work. The Sabbath represents leaving that bondage, both literally and figuratively. We leave the work week behind, we shed our work clothes, our cell phones, our computers, and enter into a different reality. Every week on the seventh day, we are very much leaving Egypt, just as we left it thousands of years ago.

It is interesting to note that the word "religion" does not appear in the Torah. (It was only said once, by our enemy

Haman, and he was greatly mistaken.) Judaism is not a religion, it is a *relationship*. It is God reaching out to us to have a relationship with Him through our daily actions. The same way in our relationship with our spouses, children, and friends, it is difficult to communicate to the ones we love the most while we are busy talking or texting someone else, so too in our relationship to God. On the Sabbath, we turn off our cell phones, our computers, our cars, and we focus on the one relationship in the world that means the most.

In our prayer services, the Sabbath is allegorically compared to a beautiful queen and bride. One of the great Talmudic sages used to wrap himself in his cloak and say, "Come, let us go and greet the Sabbath Queen." The great Kabbalist Rabbi Shlomo HaLevi Alkabetz composed one of the great songs that we sing as part of the Friday night prayer service. The chorus of this song is, "Come my Beloved to greet the bride, Let us welcome the Sabbath." At the highlight of the song we turn around to face the door as if to greet a bride and sing "Enter in peace, O crown of her husband, even in gladness and good cheer, among the faithful of the treasured nation enter O Bride! Enter O Bride!" This is the spirit with which we enter the Sabbath.

This is why many have the custom to recite the Song of Songs on the eve of the Sabbath. The Song of Songs is an allegory of the special bond that two lovers have to each other is similar to the love God has for the Jewish People. The parable is about two lovers who have been separated and long for each other before finally seeing each other again. The feeling of joy overwhelms both of them. This is similar to the Jewish People who are, to a certain extent away from God all week long and finally are reunited on the Sabbath day.

The Sabbath Bliss

There is no greater joy in the world that can be reached than what a Jew can feel on the Sabbath. On the Sabbath, the Talmud tells us, we receive an extra soul. This is because the level that we can reach is so high, that one soul is not enough. The height that a Jew can reach on the Sabbath is beyond extraordinary. The Talmud writes that the Sabbath is one sixtieth of the World to Come. What does this mean? Rabbi Akiva Tatz explains that in Jewish Law one sixtieth is always the borderline measurement. For example, if a piece of non-kosher meat fell into a pot that has kosher food in it, if the non-kosher piece makes up less than one sixtieth of the total food, then one can eat from the pot. This is because the non-kosher meat is nullified to the kosher meat in this mixture. However, if the non-kosher meat makes up greater than one sixtieth, it is not nullified and the mixture may *not* be eaten. This is because this amount is the borderline of whether or not it can be tasted. So too it is with the Sabbath, if one does not try to experience it, it is a meaningless day full of restrictions. However, if one does experience it, it is a taste of Eternity.

Central to Our Faith

The Sabbath has always been a central tenet to the Jewish Faith. It is one of the Ten Commandments. In Biblical times, one would incur the death penalty for violating the laws of the Sabbath. During a week, we say at the morning a prayer for that day of the week. However, instead of saying "This is the Tuesday Prayer" or "The Wednesday Prayer" we say "This is the Prayer for the third day *since the Sabbath*" or "The fourth day *since the Sabbath*." Thus we see that the Sabbath is the highlight of the week and the entire week center around it.

There is a story told of one simple Jew named Chatzkele who was a porter and would carry the food during the week in honor of the Sabbath. As he carried the food he would gleefully sing, "I am carrying this in honor of the Sabbath!" Chatzkele was considered a hidden *tzaddik* despite his simplicity since everything he did was for the sake of the Sabbath.

In Talmudic times, the Sages used to go to any lengths to buy the choicest meat for the Sabbath, but there is a story of one sage who was poor and could not afford more expensive meat. What did he do? He chopped his vegetables in thinner slices for the Sabbath just to make the meal more elaborate and set it apart from the rest of the week. In the *Shulchan Aruch* (Code of Jewish Law) it is written that we should make every attempt to beautify the Sabbath. Many people buy exquisite foods, fine chinaware, and white tablecloths to enhance the Sabbath experience.

What is so special about the Sabbath? What makes it so holy? What does it commemorate? And what does the Torah mean when it says "Desist from work?"

The Dual Aspect of the Sabbath

Rabbi Aryeh Kaplan writes a great deal about the significance of the Sabbath. He writes that there are several different times when the Torah mentions the commandment to honor the Sabbath. One is surrounding the creation of the world in the Book of Genesis. The other times are in the Books of Exodus and Deuteronomy when the Ten Commandments are enumerated.

In the Book of Exodus, the central theme surrounding the Sabbath seems to be symbolic of the seventh day in which God "rested" after creating the earth. This is as it says, "You shall do no manner of work... For in six days, God made heaven and earth and sea and all that is in them, and He rested on the seventh day. Therefore, God blessed the Sabbath day and made it holy."

However, in the Book of Deuteronomy it is written "Observe the Sabbath day and keep it holy as God commanded you…. And you shall remember that you were a slave in Egypt and God took you out with a mighty hand and an outstretched arm. Therefore, God commanded you to keep the Sabbath day."

In this passage, it appears that the primary theme of observing the Sabbath is meant to commemorate leaving the bondage of slavery in Egypt. How are we to reconcile these two very different themes behind Sabbath observance?

Rabbi Aryeh Kaplan gives a most ingenious answer. There are two aspects of God that are fundamental to our beliefs. The first is the recognition that He is the Creator Who fashioned the entire universe into being. The second aspect, which is perhaps even more significant, is that God still plays an active role in our daily lives. This was demonstrated most compellingly when God took us out from servitude in Egypt amidst great and spectacular miracles. The Exodus remains a central tenet to Jewish Faith that God takes an active role in each of our lives and cares very deeply about each of us.

On the Sabbath we commemorate these two aspects of God. We stop to commemorate the creation of the World by resting on the seventh day as God rested on the seventh day. We also remember that God took an active role in our daily lives by sanctifying us into a nation through the Exodus, and so we sanctify the seventh day and make it holy.

As mentioned before there is a deeper comparison between the Sabbath and the Exodus. On the Exodus, we were taken out of bondage and servitude and brought into real freedom. This is strikingly similar to the Sabbath. On the Sabbath we leave the six days of servitude behind. We throw away our shackles that bind us to materialism and pettiness and once again experience freedom. True Freedom allows our spirit to soar unrestrained. This is the true secret of the Sabbath. It is no coincidence that the Talmud writes that the Torah was given on the Sabbath, for through receiving the Torah we experienced what true freedom is.

What does it mean in the Torah to "desist from work on the Sabbath"? What does "work" mean? The concept of labor is derived from the passage in the Torah concerning the building of the *Mishkan* (Tabernacle). In the middle of discussing the importance of constructing the Tabernacle, the Torah suddenly writes that it is important to observe the Sabbath and refrain from doing labor. Why did the Torah choose here to remind us not to perform any labor on the Sabbath? The Talmud explains that all of the labors involved in constructing the Tabernacle were forbidden on the Sabbath and the laws of the Sabbath override the importance of building the Tabernacle. This means that it was forbidden to continue with construction of the Tabernacle on the Sabbath. This is how we derive the 39 forbidden labors on the Sabbath for all of them were used in the construction of the Tabernacle. For example, spinning, dying, and sewing are forbidden because all of these labors were used to make the curtains used in the Tabernacle. One of the common misconceptions is that work means exertion and physical labor. However, this cannot be, for many of the labors that we are to refrain from take very little effort at all. For example, writing and untying are two of the forbidden labors, both of which take very little effort.

Why were the prohibitions taken specifically from labor involved in building the Tabernacle? What connection is there between the Tabernacle and the Sabbath? Rabbi Aryeh Kaplan explains that the Talmudic Sages call the Tabernacle a microcosm for all of creation. The Tabernacle represented man's responsibility to elevate creation by developing a connection with God. The *Midrash* writes that in this sense, man's building of the Tabernacle parallels God's creation of the world. Thus by refraining from working on the Tabernacle, one is commemorating God's rest from creating the world.

Furthermore, I would say that there are essentially two dimensions in which we serve God; the dimension of time and of space. The *sukkah* and synagogue for example represent the dimension of space and the festivals represent the dimension of time. Sabbath and the Tabernacle is the pinnacle of serving God in the dimensions of time and space. Thus we see that the Sabbath takes precedence over the most importance structure in the physical world; namely the Tabernacle.

What is special about these 39 labors that we refrain from on the Sabbath? Rabbi Samson Raphael Hirsch explains that each of these labors represents man's mastery over nature. For example, harvesting and plowing represent man's mastery over the world of agriculture. These are why these two labors are forbidden on the Sabbath. During the six days of the week, we can lose sight of who is the real creator of Nature when we manipulate Nature to serve our needs. The Sabbath is the time when we remember that ultimately God is the Creator of all Nature and everything is subject to His will.

Giving Someone the Gift of the Sabbath

One way in which we could taste the Sabbath is by giving the Sabbath to someone else. *Rabbi* Shlomo Carlebach tells the story of one simple Jew named Moshe Dovid who was absolutely destitute. One day he decided the only way he would be able to support his family would be to save up enough money (500 rubles) to buy a farm. For years, Moshe Dovid and his family starved themselves till they finally had the 500 rubles to buy a farm. It was Friday and Moshe Dovid traveled to the marketplace to buy a farm. He realized he did not have enough time to buy a farm before the Sabbath began, and he knew that one is forbidden to carry money on the Sabbath. So what did he do? He knocked on the door of the holy Chernovitzer, the great Rebbe of that city. There he knew the money would be safe. As he was about to give the money to the Chernovitzer, a woman walked in sobbing uncontrollably. The Chernovitzer tried to comfort her, but the woman would not be consoled. She said, "I am a widow, my husband just passed away. My daughter is supposed to get married right after the Sabbath. Unfortunately we don't have the means to pay for the wedding. If the groom finds out that we cannot pay for the wedding, the wedding will not take place!" She was crying bitter tears.

Right away Moshe Dovid pulled out the 500 rubles to give to the woman. The Chernovitzer tried to stop him. "No!" he exclaimed. "Your family needs the money. This is what you have been saving for years. Don't do this."

But Moshe Dovid wouldn't listen. He turned to the woman and said, "I can always resave the money and buy a farm one day. But as for you, who know if your daughter will ever be able to find someone else who she loves? *Mazel Tov* on the wedding." And with that, he handed her the money.

The Chernovitzer turned to Moshe Dovid and smiled, "My pure and precious Moshe Dovid. God will make you rich beyond your dreams goes without saying. However, beyond this, I want to wish you something so special. Do you know what kind of a Sabbath this poor woman and her daughter would have had if you hadn't given them the money? Can you imagine the poor widow without her husband, knowing after the Sabbath she would have to cancel the wedding? Can you imagine the poor daughter without a husband, wondering if she would ever be able to get married? *But you*, Moshe Dovid gave the Sabbath to two people. Therefore, I bless you, God should give you the Sabbath all of your life."

From that point on, Moshe Dovid experienced the Sabbath like no one else in the world. Every Friday night he would glow with the Sabbath bliss. Everyone would notice how Moshe Dovid radiated with joy on the Sabbath.

This story illustrates that the greatest way to experience the Sabbath is to give the Sabbath to someone else. How can one do this? By teaching someone who has never experienced the Sabbath before what the Sabbath is all about. One does this by inviting them over on Friday night and have them experience firsthand what has bonded the Jewish People together for thousands of years.

The Talmud refers to the time when the Messiah will come as a time when all will be a complete Sabbath. What does this mean? There will be a day when closeness to God will be felt so strongly, that everyone all over the world will experience the bliss of Sabbath on the deepest level. Until then, every Sabbath serves as a reminder of the Great Sabbath that has yet to come.

Rabbi Moshe Weinberger tells a story about the holy Rizhner. Jews used to come from far and wide to receive blessings from the great Rizhner. One Jew, who had terrible pain and sadness in his life, waited for several hours to receive a blessing from the Rizhner. When he came out, one of the Rizhner's disciples asked him what the Rizhner told him. He answered, "God should give me strength to recover from this suffering." "That's it?" the disciple asked incredulously. "That the best the Rizhner can tell you? What are you expected to do until that point? You have to wait on line and ask him what can he do you for right now in the meantime!" The man agreed and waited on line again. When he came out for the second time, the disciple asked again, "What did the Rizhner tell you this time?" The man replied "God should give me strength until he gives me strength."

Rabbi Weinberger says that there is a profound lesson to be learned from this simple story. The day will come when God will give us the real strength, the strength we have all been waiting for. That day will be the day when the Messiah comes. However, until that point, the Sabbath is God giving us a little strength until He comes down and really give us strength. Let us all experience Sabbath fully each week and prepare us for that Great Day when all will be Sabbath.

Spiritual Exercises

1. Try to think of a moment when you felt the beauty of the Sabbath. What was special about that moment? Can it be duplicated each week?

2. Try to think of a moment when you felt a need to escape the physical materialistic world. What made you want to escape? Does the Sabbath help you alleviate that feeling?

3. Imagine a world where every day is the same, when the seventh day of the week is no different than the rest of the week. How do you think you would feel?

4. Try to think of ways to make your Sabbath more beautiful and meaningful, whether through singing a Sabbath song, studying Torah, or a saying a meaningful Sabbath prayer. Try to refrain from mundane activities that would make your Sabbath feel empty.

5. Try to spend a few minutes each Sabbath closing your eyes and thinking about the beauty of the day. Then try to monitor how this affects your Sabbath as well as how it changes your life.

Chapter 13
The Inner Light of Chassidut

Of diamonds in the Lord's crown, the costliest,
Shining jewel of humility,
In modesty the purest,
Source of peace and loyalty,
In faith the deepest.
To him, thousands of Jacob's sheep have hastened,
Through him their thirsty souls have quenched,
And to his wisdom piously have listened,
Our teacher and our master godly man perfected,
Light of all Israel eternally ahead.

~ The Holy Rabbi Sholom of Belz

OVER TWO HUNDRED YEARS AGO, a new fire was unleashed into the world. This was the fire brought down into the world by the great Rabbi Israel Baal Shem Tov. A new path to serve God was forged. The Jewish People would never be the same again.

The name Baal Shem Tov literally means, "Master of the Good Name." Why was he given this name? Many have said that it is because the great Israel spread the word of God in a positive way all over the world and once again gave God, so to speak a good name. The Jewish People were reeling from unspeakable persecution and torture, having recently experienced the Massacres of 1648 and 1649 and countless other pogroms throughout Europe. The Jewish People needed to once again feel happy about being Jewish, and that was exactly what the Baal Shem Tov gave them.

There is another reason why Rabbi Israel was given this title. When a person wakes someone up from a sleep he whispers the name of the person softly in the sleeping person's ear and says, "Get up, it's time to wake up." This is what The Baal Shem Tov did. He whispered the Jewish People's name "Israel" softly in their ear and said. "Get up, it's time to wake up." It was time for the deep spiritual slumber which has enveloped them for so long after experiencing so much pain and sadness. It was time to end the dreary, rote, and cold rituals that sadly enough Judaism had become. It was time to sing, dance, and pray again. It was time to give hope and joy to the common, simple Jew who struggled all week long to provide food for his family.

The Baal Shem Tov descended into the world.

A mystical figure that spent many years meditating in the Carpathian Mountains, the Baal Shem Tov focused on the study of the Talmud, the primary book of study at the time, but he cared much more for the Kabbalah. In accordance with the teaching that "the Torah is written in the language of man," he spoke in a new invigorating way that appealed to the masses. He taught that the greatest way to love God is to love your fellow man. Soon, his reputation as a holy man and healer spread. Moreover, the Baal Shem Tov represented a new type of energy to the Jewish World. While the world of Kabbalah spoke to the elite scholars, the Chassidic movement spoke to the simple man. For centuries, Kabbalah was an esoteric subject forbidden by many, and understood by few. Now many of the deep Kabbalistic ideas contained in the Torah was accessible by man.

Differences Between Chassidut and Kabbalah

One of the students of the Seer of Lublin, a great Chassidic master, was once asked how the Chassidic movement differed from the Kabbalistic movement, in Safed in the fifteenth and sixteenth centuries. The student answered as follows:

> A hunter once returned to his hometown describing a bird he had never seen before. The bird was exquisitely beautiful, with wings of many colors, and flew higher and faster than any bird he had ever seen. Moreover, the bird had an angelic voice that somehow soothed him in a way he had never felt before. Mystified, most of the people in the town did not believe him. Some time went by and another hunter returned from the forest with a similar story, but this time described the bird with more human like features. Still few people believed him. More time went by without any new sightings of the bird. Finally, a third hunter came and brought the bird to the people. Alas, the story was believed.

The parable is a reference to the story of Kabbalistic thought. The bird represents Kabbalah, for it is the one creature which can fly to the heavens, yet lives here on earth, the merging of the Upper and Lower realms. Many years ago Rabbi Shimon Bar Yochai, the author of the Zohar, a primary part of Kabbalah, came to the world. However, few people understood or believed its deep messages. Centuries later, a young mystic Rabbi Isaac Luria (the Arizal) continued with the Zohar's teachings; however, it was still difficult to grasp by the multitudes. Finally, the Ball Shem Tov came and brought the bird to the people, and at last it was understood.

This idea is further illustrated in another parable said by Rabbi Shneur Zalman Liadi. The parable is as follows:

There was once a king whose son fell ill with a serious life-threatening illness. No doctor in the land could revive the child. Finally, a doctor in herbal medicine stepped forward and after examining the boy, said he believed he knew what could cure him. He said that he needed a 28-karat ruby gem ground to a pulp mixed with some common herbs and mixed with water. This potion would save the boy.

The attendants there were shocked, for they all knew that the ruby this doctor requested was the centerpiece of the crown of the king himself. Some of the attendants were appalled that one could even suggest such a thing. Others felt that the king said his son must be saved at any cost. During the ensuing *melee*, the doctor, seized the crown of the king and extracted the precious gem. He ground it to dust, mixed it with the herbs and water and gave it to the dying prince to drink. Miraculously, the prince was saved.

This parable is very deep and contains the essence of Chassidut itself. In the parable, the king is God, the prince is the Jewish People, and the herbal doctor is the Baal Shem Tov. The Jewish People were dying, reeling from persecution and assimilation. When no other medicine worked, the Baal Shem Tov came and blazed a new trail to revive his people. He seized the centerpiece of God's crown, so to speak, the *Sod,* the secrets of the Torah. This was the ancient wisdom of the Kabbalah. However, he first ground them into a fine pulp and mixed it with water. This means he made the deepest teachings most palpable to the common folk. He taught the most beautiful Torah in a way that everyone can relate to and understand.

Difference Between
Chassidut & Traditional Judaism

How does Chassidic thought differ from traditional observant Judaism? One of the many ways can also be illustrated with the following parable:

> A Chassid decided to collect money for his Chassidic town. He dressed as an ordinary Jew and went to a nearby *Mitnaged* (Those who opposed Chassidut) town for the weekend. Once in the town, he used all the guises of the *Mitnagdim* in order not to arouse suspicion. He told the people in the town that he came from a town that was very poor and that he was sent to collect money. Many of the people in the town were fooled by the man's appearance. However, one person in the town suspected that the man was a Chassid. He called over the Chassid and asked him, "So tell me what you think of Chassidim."
>
> The Chassid waved his hand dismissively. "All Chassidim seem to do is talk about food and money. They seem to have no interest in spiritual matters. However, in the *Mitnaged* town, they are always talking about spiritual matters."
>
> The man was satisfied that this person could not be a Chassid for he would not speak in such a derogatory manner about Chassidim. He gave the Chassid some money and bade him farewell.
>
> When the Chassid returned home, word somehow spread about what the Chassid said about Chassidim.

People in the town were very angry. How could the Chassid speak so badly about his own people?

This is what the Chassid replied, "It is the nature of people to speak about a novelty. People are always speaking about something that is new and exciting to them. For the *Mitnaged*, it is a given that there is a physical world which we are a part of. The novelty is that there is also a God who runs the world. So they are constantly talking about God and spiritual matters.

"However, to the Chassid, it is so obvious that there is a God and He gave us the Torah. The novelty is that there is also a physical world out there as well! That is why a Chassid talks a great deal about the physical world; the spiritual world is completely obvious and does not to be discussed."

The Real World, The Inner World

This is one of the great differences between the Chassidic world and the non-Chassidic world. For the true Chassid, the world of the spirit is very much the real world and this world is little more than an illusion. The world is most real on the inside, which cannot be seen but only experienced.

The previous Lubavitcher Rebbe spent a long time in a Soviet prison. During this time, the Soviets tried desperately to get the Rebbe to violate the laws of Judaism, but he steadfastly refused. Once a Soviet officer put a gun right up to the Rebbe's forehead and threatened to shoot if the Rebbe still refused to obey his commands. Incredibly, the Rebbe laughed at him, "What would you be taking away from me? You can take this world away from me, but the next one is far better and more real, and that world you can never take away."

This is why Rabbi Nachman of Breslov, who was in excruciating pain from tuberculosis, remained very calm when he lay on his deathbed. He told his disciples that leaving this world was just like going from one corridor into the next, and there was nothing to fear.

For many, this approach takes one away from all of the bleak intoxications of this world and takes us into a world of hope and exuberance. Suddenly, all of the trials and tribulations of this world are put into an entirely different perspective. It is not that this world is negated completely in favor of the next world. It is that this world is a *process*, a journey, which brings us to the next world. In *Pirkei Avot* we are taught this world is a vestibule for the next world, and we must prepare ourselves to enter the banquet hall, so that we can partake of the feast. While this world matters tremendously, it takes on infinitely more significance if looked at as a process. Along the way, God gives us, as Rabbi Nachman calls them 'road marks' along the path to guide us to our date with destiny.

It is written in Proverbs, "The candle of God is the soul of man." The first Lubavitcher Rebbe, Rabbi Shneur Zalman Liadi, explained this passage beautifully. There is always the part of the flame which is attached to the wick, the physical part within man. However, the flame is also always striving to move upward. It is in this way that we are God's candle; our body remains attached to the wick, but our soul is striving to reach a higher place. This idea is really rooted in Judaism itself, but is emphasized much more in Chassidut. We are living in this world, but at the same time reaching for more. There is a part of us that is ethereal.

The world of the Chassid, as mentioned before, is the world of the inside, the world that cannot be seen. This world is far greater than the outside world, the world we do see. We find a source for this idea in a startling Midrash.

Deeper Meaning to the Mitzvot

Moreover Chassidut emphasizes finding the meaning behind the *mitzvot* as a precursor to their fulfillment. While the *Sefer HaChinnuch* writes that "man is formed by his actions," Chassidut takes a somewhat opposite approach. It is only when one *understands the significance* of the *mitzvot* that one can be brought to action. The Kotzker Rebbe once said a very thought provoking statement. He stated, "There are no real fast days in Judaism. It is more that on Yom Kippur who *wants* to eat and on *Tisha B'Av* who *can* eat." What this means is that if we were to really understand the *significance* of these days; that on Yom Kippur God is looking each one of our actions and that on *Tisha B'Av* we are commemorating two thousand years of Jewish tragedies, we would never eat on those days. This means that in reality, *halachah*, Jewish Law is not laws which bring us to a state of higher consciousness, but rather *halachah* is an outgrowth of our own national spiritual expression. This is the dimension of Chassidut, passion in fulfilling the *mitzvot* through understanding their meaning. This does not include those *mitzvot* that we don't understand the reason for them, such as *sha'atnez,* the commandment not to wear wool and linen together. However, the *mitzvot* that we do understand, understanding must always come first, and only then can we be led to action.

The Greatness in Man

Another difference between Chassidic thought and traditional Jewish thought is the focus on man's greatness. Unlike the *Mussar* movement, which emphasized correcting the faults and weaknesses within man, the Chassidic movement focused on the strength and potential within man. Man was not something to be degraded, and meant to be filled with shame and humiliation, but lifted up, encouraged, and inspired.

This difference could be seen from the following short anecdote. A man was once seen after the morning prayers with his *tefillin* on while fixing his wagon wheel. A *Mitnaged* rabbi saw this and immediately started rebuking the man. "How dare you fix your wagon wheel while wearing your *tefillin? Tefillin* are something which are holy, and your are just callously wearing them as you do an ordinary mundane act!"

At that moment a Chassidic rabbi walked by. When he saw this same man, he shook his head with admiration. He exclaimed, "Wow, look at how special the Jewish People are! Even when they fix their wagon wheel, they wear their *tefillin*, showing that even during simple mundane acts their thoughts are on God!"

What a radically different approach to Judaism, God, and Man!

Another great aspect of Chassidut is its approach to how to view the simple unlearned individual. Until this point, the only person in the Jewish community that was given honor was the scholar. Simple people were often ignored or looked down at while the scholar was elevated to a higher stature. The Baal Shem Tov taught that this was not the way. Even the simple folk could get close to God, and often in their simplicity can be raised to an even more exalted level than the scholar.

A famous story about the Baal Shem Tov occurred one Yom Kippur night. Everyone in the synagogue was praying fervently for the atonement of their sins. One simple shepherd boy, who did not know how to pray pulled out his flute and began to play. Mortified, the members of the congregation began to push him out of the synagogue for it was forbidden to play the flute on Yom Kippur. The Baal Shem Tov immediately stopped them. "Till this point, every one's prayers have only reached the Heavenly Gates," he declared. "However, this boy's prayers went straight till the throne."

Thus Chassidut starts from the inside; from simplicity and purity, not from intellectual scholarship. It was this vision that won the hearts of the common folk and caused Chassidut to take Europe by storm.

A Personal Relationship with God

Another beautiful aspect of Chassidut is the emphasis on developing a real intimate relationship with our Creator. The great Rabbi Levi Yitzchak of Berditchev used to converse with God openly while he prayed, often in layman's terms. He even demanded sometimes to be able to understand hardships and why the Jewish People had to suffer so much. In Chassidic thought, God is not an abstract being too lofty and awesome to converse with. Rather God is very real and very much a part of our lives and a true Friend, so to speak, which we can talk to and can comfort us in our time of need.

Also, there is the emphasis on the story, and their deeper meaning. But first, a word of caution about stories in general, in particular the Chassidic story. All leaders, no matter how great they may be, always have shortcomings. No story, no matter how wonderful and inspiring it may be, should in any way deify one of our leaders (one of the big differences between Judaism and Christianity lies within this idea). For a leader is not superhuman. A leader is someone who is very much human, but at times rises to perform superhuman acts. It isn't about being perfect; it is about being in fact, very imperfect, but at times *rising* to levels of perfection. True inspiration admits to our humanness, all of the greatest leaders in the Written Book had flaws, but in spite of the flaws accomplished extraordinary things.

While there are certainly many stories of the great Rabbis and leaders in the *Mitnaged* world, it is in Chassidut that the emphasis is placed on the story itself as a way to teach great lessons. In a Chassidic story we see very often the humanness of the great leaders and their ability to speak to God as one would speak to a friend. We see the great celebrated Rabbi Levi Yitzchak of Berditchev, often known as the Berditchever, confronting God sometimes openly in the synagogue, sometimes bargaining with God and at times even accusing God, but all done for the sake of the Jewish People, for the Berditchiver's love for his people knew no bounds. Sometimes these stories focus on very regular every day actions, how a Rebbe ate, how he slept or even went to the bathroom. We see the deep seated love each of the Rebbes had for every individual Jew, no matter what their background or level of knowledge. Some of these stories are quite fantastical, some are whimsical, exaggerated, or perhaps even entirely untrue, but they are always there to teach us a lesson about ourselves.

The story is told about a Rebbe who was approached by a Chassid asking for a blessing. This Chassid had no money, no children, and was in poor health. Sadly enough, the Rebbe told him the Gates of Heaven were closed and a blessing would have no effect in this world. As the Chassid got back into his wagon and started to leave, he looked out the window and saw the Rebbe chasing after his wagon. He stopped the wagon and allowed the Rebbe to catch up, huffing and puffing, clearly out of breath. When he could speak, the Rebbe said to him, "It is true that the Gates of heaven are right now closed, but I can still cry with you."

The Chassid got out of the wagon, and the two of them hugged and wept openly on each other's shoulders. As the tears were spilling onto the Chassid's coat, the Rebbe turned to him and said, "Wow! We just opened the Gates of Heaven!"

I love this story for many reasons. It contains all of the elements of the classic Chassidic tale; the despondent Chassid turning to his Rebbe for help and the Rebbe responding in kind. It is the simplicity of the story that reveals its depth. Here we see all of the elements, the very human and emotional experience of both the Rebbe and the Chassid. We also see the sensitivity of the Rebbe and his love for the Chassid, his candid answer to the Chassid, and the ability to change what is taking place in Heaven by our actions and prayers.

Finally, we turn to what in my opinion is the greatest contribution of all, and that is that Chassidut helped to transform Jewish worship into unbridled passion. Before Chassidut, Judaism felt dry, intellectual, scholarly, and rigid. Chassidut changed that completely. Rabbi Shlomo Carlebach, who was deeply connected to the thought and teachings of Chassidut, always put a great emphasis on getting close to God with real enthusiasm, and ecstasy. "When it comes to Judaism," he would often say, "You have to take it to the very end. You could either pray by just turning the pages in the prayerbook, or you could storm the Gates of Heaven." This is the message that Chassidut brought to the world.

The Berditchever once stood up in his synagogue, and screamed out, "My fellow Jews! Whatever you do, always remember that there is a Father in Heaven!" My personal prayer for us all is that we experience Chassidut the way it was meant to be experienced, the deep personal relationship we can have with God, and all of the longing and joy one can experience when getting close to our Father in Heaven.

Spiritual Exercises

1. Try to remember a time when you felt connected to Judaism in a deep meaningful way. What was it that made you feel that way?

2. Try to take a little time to learn about some of the great Chassidic masters. Some of the most commonly studied biographies are Rabbi Nachman of Breslov, the Baal Shem Tov, Rabbi Levi Yitzchak of Berditchev, Reb Shneur Zalman of Liadi, and the previous Lubavitcher Rebbe, Rabbi Menachem Mendel Schneerson. Much can be learned from studying the lives of great people.

3. Try to take a few minutes each day to read through some of the writings of the great Chassidic masters. Many of their works have been translated into English, and are easily accessible. Then document how you feel and how your life feels after studying their writings.

Chapter 14
Extending Your Hand

Those who make compassion an essential part of their lives find the joy of life. Kindness deepens the spirit and produces rewards that cannot be completely explained in words. It is an experience more powerful than words. To become acquainted with kindness one must be prepared to learn new things and feel new feelings. Kindness is more than a philosophy of the mind. It is a philosophy of the spirit.

~ Robert J. Furey

L ET ME RELATE TO YOU the following remarkable story told over by Harold Schultz, the CEO of Starbucks, at a dinner in his honor at Columbia School of Business. At one time in his career he traveled to Israel with a group of other CEO's. During his stay, he saw that something new had been added to his itinerary. In addition to the usual tourist hot spots, he was to visit the esteemed Rabbi Nosson Tzvi Finkel, a brilliant Torah luminary and leader of the Mirrer Yeshiva. After extensive traveling to exotic sites such as Ein Gedi and the Dead Sea, he and the other CEO's soon found themselves in a small, worn out office with a distinguished elderly sage. He suffered terribly from

Parkinson's disease, yet he refused to take any medication for fear that it would affect his mind. When he stood, he had to grip the back of his chair to steady himself. Many of the prominent businessmen averted their eyes from the painful site in front of them. He addressed them in a soft gentle voice.

"Tell, me," he asked them. "What is the greatest moral lesson that can be learned from the Holocaust?" No one answered at first, so he called on one of them. "To never forget?" the man responded meekly. Rabbi Finkel waved his hand dismissively. He called on someone else. "The sheep shall not go meekly to the slaughter?" the man answered in an unsteady voice. Once again, Rabbi Finkel waved off this clichéd answer. "Does anyone here know?" Everyone looked down at the floor, unsure what to answer, seemingly afraid to be called on.

Rabbi Finkel leaned forward. "The answer to this question is in how the people reacted to their predicament. After the Jews were stuffed into the cattle cars and taken to the concentration camps, the Nazi guards in their sadism would bring one blanket to one person, per floor on each level of the barrack. The problem was that there were six people on each row. This person then had to make a choice. Does he keep the blanket for himself, or does he look beyond his own pain and share it with the five others, even though he knew it would mean he would shiver himself? The Nazis believed every person was deep down essentially an animal, and this simple test would reveal each person's deep down selfish, instinctual, and animalistic nature. However, nearly always, the person chose to share it with others. This is the greatest lesson of the Holocaust, the power of the human spirit. Man, and only man, has the ability to rise above his physical body, and truly learn to give." His voice dropped to a whisper. "When you go back to America, take your blanket and share it with five others."

What an extraordinary lesson from an extraordinary person about what it means to share what we have with others. All other creatures live in the world of instinct and live primarily to take from this world. Man, and Man alone, has the ability to rise above this base instinct, and have the ability to give. This is the greatness of Man.

The Greatest Way to Get Close to God

It is interesting to note that although we say blessings on all of the *mitzvot* prior to their performance, there are no blessings recited over acts of kindness. For example, we say no blessings on giving charity. We say no blessings for honoring our parents. We say no blessings for visiting the sick. Why is this so? These were commanded to us by God just as shaking a *lulav,* or sitting in a *sukkah?* So why do we only say blessings concerning our relationship to man, but not concerning our relationship to our fellow man?

There is a beautiful answer from Rabbi Yechiel Yaakov Weinberg which answers this idea. He discusses why we do not say a blessing on giving *shalach manot,* which is a mitzvah mandated in the Book of Esther to give fruit baskets to our friends and neighbors on the holiday of Purim. He explains that the reason we don't say a blessing is because simply doing the mitzvah arouses within us a sense of love for our fellow man. That means to a certain extent, we are doing this not because we were commanded to do it, but because this reaches deep within us and allows us to express our love for humanity in a way that is beyond the commandment.

Paradoxically, by leaving God out of the equation, by *not* making a blessing on acts of kindness, we are expressing our love for God in an even deeper way. By expressing our love for our fellow man, we are recognizing the divine image within Man; we are recognizing that each one of us is an extension of Him. Thus by leaving God out of the equation, ironically we are recognizing Him even more. We are in the process developing a stronger relationship to Him.

We are taught that from the patriarchs and matriarchs how we can learn how to lead our lives: "The actions of our forefathers are a sign for the children." We see the power of kindness from none other than the father of the Jewish People, Abraham himself. The Bible talks about Abraham sitting at the entrance of his tent waiting to greet guests. At the moment when three guests arrived, God was in the middle of speaking to Abraham. Incredibly, Abraham interrupted God and ran out to greet the three guests! Not only is Abraham not chastised for this, on the contrary he is exalted for it. The Talmud tells us we learn from this, "Kindness is even greater than the revealing of the Divine Presence."

What does it mean to give to another person?

Ever since we were little children we were taught about the importance of kindness. "Help an old lady cross the street," our parents would say. "Give charity to people in need." "Offer a kind word to someone who is sad."

Emulating God's Ways

Why? What is so special about the power of giving? The Torah teaches us why it is so special to give. In Deuteronomy we are taught, "And you shall walk in His ways." This means that there is a commandment to try to emulate God's ways. The Talmud says, "Just as God is merciful, so too you shall be merciful." Why is it so important to emulate God's ways? What is the purpose of this commandment?

The answer to this question teaches us one of the most fundamental tenets of Judaism. God is above and beyond the physical world. Moses, the greatest of all prophets tried to understand God, but was not able to understand

Him. "No man shall see Me and live," God responded. So how does one get close to a Being that he or she cannot understand? Herein lies the answer; by emulating His ways. When I was a little child, I looked up to my brother. I wanted him to like me. However, I knew that he wouldn't like me, for he was too big and cool for me. The only way I perceived he would notice me and like me is through acting like him. He was a Yankees and Celtics fan, so I decided to root for those teams. I dressed like him and tried to talk like him.

This is essentially what we are doing when we emulate God's ways. In our own small way, we are trying to develop a relationship with him, by imitating His ways. Moreover, we are fulfilling the role for which we were created. This answer should suffice; however, there is even more to this idea. By giving to another person, we are recognizing the Godly spark within him or her. We are saying that we understand their worth, the unique soul that they have been given. This power to see that spark is tapping into not only their Godliness, but ours as well. We remember God, who has given us so much, and is constantly sustaining us with His kindness. Rabbi David Aron points out that this is why the famous verse in the Torah, "Love your neighbor as yourself," concludes with the words, "I am God." For it is through recognizing God that we can appreciate caring for others, for we see the Godliness within man, and through giving to others, we are giving to Him.

Pirkei Avot places so much emphasis on the virtues of kindness. "The world stands on three pillars: Torah, Service (Prayer), and Acts of Kindness." When we learn Torah, we are connecting to God's will. When we pray, we are connecting our will to His will. When we perform acts of kindness, we are fulfilling His will. This is why the Talmud teaches us that it is action, not study which is the highest form of worship. For study is merely stating the goal, action is fulfilling the goal. Moreover the act of giving changes a person. The person has reached beyond themselves through caring for another person.

Kindness Holds Up the World

We see the power of kindness in the story of Noah. Noah lived in a world that was full of corruption. God decreed that the world should be destroyed with a flood; however he and his family's lives were spared, and the Torah calls him a *tzaddik*, a righteous person.

We find a startling *Midrash* by the story of Noah. The Midrash writes that all of the days when Noah was in the ark, he had to spend all of his time acting as a zookeeper, feeding the animals. In fact, according to the Midrash, when Noah was once late with feeding the lion, the lion bit Noah in anger! The question is, why did Noah have to spend his time working on such a menial task? God was already performing open miracles in the ark, such as that the food never ran out and all of the animals were able to fit into such a small space! Why didn't God just perform one more miracle; namely that the animals were all able to be fed by themselves? And why did poor Noah have to be punished that he was bit by a lion when he was late for feeding it?

The answer is it is important to know and understand what was taking place inside of that ark. The world as we know it was being destroyed for its selfishness, *Ki malah ha-aretz chamas*, "the world was full of corruption." The world was corrupt to the point where people were stealing from each other constantly. Everyone was into only one thing; taking, taking, taking.

God wanted to show Noah that the new world, the world Noah was creating inside of the ark had to be different, completely different. What was taking place inside of the ark was going to be a microcosm of what the new world would be. The New World had to be built on giving, constant giving and giving selflessly: *olam chesed yibbaneh*, "the world is built on kindness." Noah was tasked with overseeing the transition from the corruption of the old world to kindness of the new one. Noah needed to be *trained* in the art of giving. And what better time than when he was in the ark as the world was being destroyed, so it could then be recreated? Man's actions, as we will see are the fundamental building blocks of the world, and therefore choosing to giving is constantly recreating the world in a positive way.

Rabbi Joseph B. Soloveitchik wrote that the actions we choose in this world are even greater than God's actions. We see this from two of the most famous mountains in the Bible: Mount Sinai and Mount Moriah. Mount Sinai was the site of the greatest revelation in history; God revealed himself to an entire people amid fire and thunder as He gave his People the Torah. Mount Moriah was the mountain where Abraham was willing to offer his beloved son Isaac as a sacrifice because God had commanded him to. Which of these two mountains is more famous today? Ironically, Mount Sinai is nowhere to be found; scholars are not sure which mountain it was. Mount Moriah, on the other hand, is the site of the Temple Mount and is one of the most visited places in the world, and is regarded by Jews as the most sacred place in the world. Which site, Rabbi Soloveitchik asked, has made a greater impact to the world today? Not the site of the revelation, which was an action performed by *God*, but rather the site of the Isaac's sacrifice, an action performed by *man*. Man's actions, and by extension, man's *choices* have a far great impact than God's actions. Our choice to give to someone else in their time of need may indeed have cosmic repercussions.

Fixing the World

Moreover, by giving to someone else we are helping to perfect the world. We mentioned earlier the concept that God made this world in an unfinished state and left it to man to complete it. By man giving to others he is helping to "finish" the creation of the world. We see the potential in man in the very beginning of Genesis. As mentioned before, when God was creating the animal kingdom, the plant life, the fish, and the ocean; after each day of creation God said, "Behold, it was good." Only after the creation of man did God say, "Behold, it is *very* good." Why this sudden extra word? Indeed, because it is only man, through his or her actions, can make the world *very* good. Other creatures live by instinct alone; it is only man who can choose to give to others, thereby making the world more holy. It is written in the *Alenu* prayer, "To fix the world with the kingdom of the Almighty One." This is the mission statement of humankind.

There is a well known statement in the Talmud by the great sage Rabbi Akiva. He stated "The commandment to love one's neighbor as oneself is the greatest principle of all the commandments." Why is this so? Certainly there are many other important commandments, such as observing the Sabbath and Yom Kippur? Rabbi Shneur Zalman of Liadi explains beautifully. The entire purpose of every single commandment in the Torah is to bring us closer to God by becoming more in touch with our soul. When one realizes that the body is only to serve the soul, then the soul becomes everything. When someone is able to see the spark of Godliness in another person, he has drawn closer to God. By treating someone else as one would himself or herself, he or she is in essence seeing the spark of God in the other person. This person has gotten to the fundamental principle of the entire Torah. By extension, by giving to another person, one has put his or her Torah learning into practice. For in *Pirkei Avot* we are taught that not study, but *practice* is the essential purpose of Torah. Giving to another person means the person has left the world of Torah as mere theory, but has brought it into the world of practice.

Part of a Greater World

Rabbi David Aaron writes extensively about the last of the ten *Sefirot*, the one closest to the physical world we live in. This *Sefirah* is *Malchut*, loosely translated as Kingdom, or Kingship. Rabbi Aaron writes that at the core of the concept of *Malchut* is community consciousness. This means that to truly bring Godliness into our lives, we must realize that we are part of a greater kingdom. By giving to others we are linking ourselves to the general body of humankind, we are no longer a small singular individual, but part of a much greater whole. We do not live in an isolated bubble. Acceptance of God into our daily lives means acceptance of His kingdom as well.

It is no coincidence that the word *tzedakah*, "charity," contains within it the word *tzedek*, "justice." How is *tzedakah* related to justice? The answer is in how we perceive our roles in this world. If we perceive ourselves as just individuals only looking out for ourselves, then there is no "justice" or reason to give to someone else. What one person earns belongs to him or her. But if one perceives of himself as just a small part of a much greater whole, of a world around us where others are less fortunate than ourselves, one begins to understand that our money was a privilege given to us, and it is for us to share with others. This is understanding justice in the fullest sense of the word; the surplus we have should be shared with others who were given much less in life.

There is a verse in the Torah about giving charity. It is written "Tithe, you shall tithe." Why the double wording? The Talmud explains the verse homiletically; "Tithe in order that you will be tithed." This means that when you give, one day you will be the recipients of gifts as well. Many take this to mean that giving to others you will lead you to become wealthy one day. However, I feel this was not what the Sages had in mind when they said this explanation. I believe they meant that through giving to others one comes to recognize and appreciate what one has. One comes to understand and be satisfied with one's lot in life, and the importance of contributing to those around us that are less fortunate. This leads a person to *feel* wealthy. In *Pirkei Avot* we are taught, "Who is wealthy? One who is satisfied with his lot." This is the same idea; true wealth is not about money in the bank account, but rather a state of mind. Through giving to others we come to appreciate what wealth really is.

The Stories of the Righteous

We can learn a great deal about the power of giving through studying the stories of *tzaddikim* (righteous people). There are many great stories of *tzaddikim* who gave of themselves to others.

A story is told that Rabbi Shneur Zalman of Liadi once desperately needed to raise money for a Jew who was being held for ransom by the neighboring Cossacks for thousands of rubles. Cossacks used to kidnap Jews and hold them for enormous ransom fees. The only one in the community who would be able to afford to pay such an exorbitant amount was a very wealthy Jew who lived on the outskirts of town. The problem was, this Jew was known to be a huge miser who never donated large amounts of money, if any money at all, to anyone.

R. Shneur Zalman decided he would go together with one of his followers to the home of this miser. The miser lived in a luxurious mansion on top of a hill, and it was a trek to even get to it. When they finally reached the home, the miser escorted them inside and listened to their tale of the poor Jew who was kidnapped and needed ransom money so he could return to his family.

The miser listened attentively and said he was sorry to hear of a Jew in such dire straits, and said he would help. He reached deep into his pockets and pulled out one ruble. This amount was probably the equivalent of a few pennies. The Chassid who had followed R. Shneur Zalman was about to rise up in indignation at receiving such a small amount. Before he could speak, however, R. Shneur Zalman stood up and hugged the miser, profusely thanking him for donating so kindly to such a worthy cause. He kept assuring the man how much his contribution meant to the community and the poor man who was being held ransom. As R. Shneur Zalman turned around and began to leave, the miser called him back. He said he could afford to give one more ruble. Once again, R. Shneur Zalman thanked the man profusely and turned once again to leave. Again, the miser stopped him and this time offered him two more rubles. R. Shneur Zalman sincerely thanked him again. This went on for quite some time, and each time the sums that the miser offered to pay grew larger and larger. Finally, R. Shneur Zalman received the entire amount needed for the ransom.

Afterward, R. Shneur Zalman turned to the disciple who was with him and explained the lesson to be learned from the incident with the miser. "Sometimes, people who have not given charity in so long are no longer used to the action of giving. By giving even a small amount, one begins to become accustomed to the habit of giving. Giving charity, like anything else, is a learned behavior. Once we start to open our hearts, it becomes easier and easier to give."

Here is another tale. This story is told about the great Rabbi Moshe Leib of Sassov, one of the early leaders of the Chassidic movement. It was near Rosh Hashanah, and it was time to say *Selichot,* the late-night or early-morning supplications said to prepare ourselves for the Day of Judgment. However, Rabbi Moshe Leib was not to be found in the synagogue. Each day passed and Rabbi Moshe Leib's seat was empty for the morning prayer. The *Mitnagdim,* those who opposed Chassidim, jeered at this. "Look!" they exclaimed. "Your great spiritual leader is sleeping in bed for he is too tired to get up early for the morning prayers!" The Chassidim responded, "This is not true. Rabbi Moshe Leib is up in Heaven during this time conversing with the angels."

As time went by, one *Mitnaged* decided to see for himself where Rabbi Moshe Leib went during the *Selichot* prayers. Early in the morning just before prayers, he went to the cabin in the woods where Rabbi Moshe Leib lived. Sure enough, he saw him sleeping in his bed. However, suddenly he awoke with a start. He quickly dressed in peasant clothes, grabbed his coat and his ax and went out the door. The *Mitnaged* followed at a safe distance, watching closely.

Rabbi Moshe Leib knocked on the door to a dilapidated cabin. An old woman answered. The *Mitnaged* recognized the woman who was a poor widow. "Yes, can I help you?"

"Well," Rabbi Moshe Leib answered. "I was just going through the woods, and I found your home. I was wondering if you needed some firewood, I would love to chop some wood for you."

"Thank you, that is very kind of you to offer."

"Sure, would love to help," Rabbi Moshe Leib responded warmly with a smile. He set out for the woods. As he swung the ax overhead he began to say the first prayer. And so he continued to say the prayers as he spent the early morning hours chopping wood for the widow.

The *Mitnaged* went back to his town, astounded by what he had just witnessed. "Is it true that Rabbi Moshe Leib goes to Heaven?" some asked him. "To Heaven?" he laughed, "if not higher."

This story, originally told by Achad Ha-Am, and retold by Elie Wiesel, contains such a powerful message. The highest way to get close to God, the furthest one can reach in Heaven is not through meditating on a mountaintop or withdrawing from the world. It is through helping our everyday man, through lifting others up, to giving and instilling hope, through caring.

Here is another tale; this one about Rabbi Meir of Premishlan. It was time for *Kiddush* on Friday night. Rabbi Meir lifted his cup and looked around the room. He paused for a minute, deep in thought. The he recited the traditional blessing over the wine. One of his disciples asked him later on what was the reason for the long pause. He answered that every time before he recites *Kiddush,* he looks at each person in the room and thinks of one good quality that each of them has. Tonight, when he came to one particular person, he could not think of any positive qualities that this man possessed. He thought very hard. Then he realized that if he was that man, he would not be attending *Kiddush* on Friday night. It was then that decided it was time to recite *Kiddush.*

Again, a simple story, but with profound meaning; the ability to see goodness inside each and every person is the first step to caring for others.

Yet another tale, this one also attributed to Rabbi Moshe Leib of Sassov. It was Simchat Torah in Sassov, the day of much rejoicing and dancing. It was an annual spectacle in the town to see the great Rebbe sing and dance with the Torah in his hands. Chassidim would fill the synagogue, all yearning to glimpse the Rebbe when he entered and watch his face glow with ecstasy.

However, one year the Rebbe did not come to synagogue. The disciples waited patiently, but when it was apparent that the Rebbe was not coming, they had no choice but to start the festivities. Many assumed the Rebbe was ill, and was not able to attend.

One Chassid believed that the Rebbe would never miss Simchat Torah with his followers unless something really urgent happened. He decided to walk to the Rebbe's home and see for himself where the Rebbe went that Simchat Torah. As he walked toward the Rebbe's home, he heard singing coming out of one of the homes. The Chassid stopped and peered into the window. He was shocked and mesmerized by what he saw; there was the celebrated Rabbi Moshe Leib of Sassov singing and dancing around this one little boy sitting in the middle of the room! He waited patiently for the dancing to end, but surprisingly it went on for hours on end. The Rabbi's face glowed as he danced around this one boy, and the Chassid noted that he seemed to be even more ecstatic than when he danced in front of hundreds of his followers. Finally, the dancing came to an end. The rabbi kissed the smiling little boy on the cheek and left.

The Chassid followed the Rabbi home. All the way, the Chassid wondered what had just taken place. Finally, he could not contain himself any longer. He went over to the Rabbi and asked, "Rabbi! With all due respect, I just witnessed you dancing in front of a little boy in his home! What was so urgent that it meant missing dancing with all of the Chassidim who looked forward to your arrival?"

Rabbi Moshe Leib smiled, "It is very simple, you see. When I was on my way to synagogue this morning, I heard crying coming out of one of the homes. Curious, I knocked on the door. No one answered. The door was open, so I went inside. It was a little boy, seated in the middle of the room, weeping softly. I asked the little boy what was wrong. He told me that his parents had gone to go see the great Rabbi Moshe Leib sing and dance with his followers. However, the boy said that he is a cripple, so he had to be left at home. When I heard this, I immediately dropped all of my plans to come to the synagogue and instead dance all seven *Hakkafot* (circuits) around this one boy."

What a lesson to be learned from this story. Giving strength to one little boy who really needed it was more important than dancing in front of all the Chassidim.

Another story, perhaps the most powerful told yet in this chapter. The celebrated sage Rabbi Aryeh Levine was well known for his remarkable acts of kindness in Palestine, prior to the creation of the State of Israel. The story goes that he was once walking with a colleague when someone approached him and asked how his cousin was doing in the mental institution. Rabbi Levine responded that he was doing well. After the man walked away, Rabbi Levine's colleague turned to Rabbi Levine with a dumbfounded look on his face. "I didn't know you had a cousin in a mental institution!"

Rabbi Levine smiled, "I really don't. Allow me to explain. I regularly visit the patients in a mental institution to give them company. During one of my visits, I noticed one patient looked terribly beaten. I asked one member of the staff why this patient was so bruised and beaten. He responded that unfortunately some of the guards take out their frustrations by beating patients in the hospital. However, the guards are afraid to harm most of the patients since they have relatives who come to visit them and the guards are afraid of any investigations. However, sadly enough, this poor patient doesn't have any relatives who come to visit him. Therefore, he bears the brunt of the guards' savagery. When I heard this, I immediately decided to adopt him as my 'cousin.' I would visit him regularly to assure that he would never be harmed. To further keep the façade, I would regularly buy him gifts when I would visit him, as many relatives do when they visit a patient. The guards believed I was his cousin and never harmed him again."

One more story about Rabbi Moshe Leib of Sassov. Rabbi Moshe Leib, who usually led the prayers on Yom Kippur night, once came an hour late to the *Kol Nidrei* prayer. When asked by his followers why he was so late to service that he was supposed to lead, he answered that on his way to the synagogue he heard a baby crying. Realizing that the baby's parents must have gone to synagogue, and so no one was home to put the baby to sleep, Rabbi Moshe Leib himself went into the home and put the baby to sleep. What an extraordinary lesson. Better to put one baby to sleep than to greet the Master of the World on the holiest day of the year.

Where do we see this concept in the Torah of the extreme precedence of kindness, even above speaking to our Creator? We see this from none other than Abraham himself. In the Book of Genesis it is written that Abraham was conversing with God when three visitors appeared at his tent. Incredibly, Abraham interrupted his communion with God to greet the visitors and feed them. Rashi says something astounding; namely we see from this that performing an act of kindness is more powerful than basking in the Divine Presence.

How far does the power of giving reach? Often, it can be felt even several generations later. A story is told about a young rabbi who wanted to begin a synagogue in Ontario.

He met with a president of a powerful bank without any referral or guarantor. The president of the bank said he cannot lend money to him, but asked out of curiosity what he needed the money for. The rabbi told him it was to build a synagogue. Surprisingly, the president suddenly said he would be happy to assist in lending the money.

The rabbi was startled. He asked what prompted this sudden change. The president confided in him the following story:

"When I was a young boy, my family was very poor. We lived near a small grocery store that was owned by a Jew. Every time my mother needed something at the store, this owner kindly let us have it for free. This went on for quite some time. Eventually I moved away, and was able to become financially secure. However, I never had a chance to repay those unbelievable acts of kindness I received as a child. Now here is my chance."

Here was an act of kindness, paid back many years later, which led to the establishment of a very large and prominent orthodox synagogue.

Another story with a similar message was once told by Rabbi Moshe Weinberger about the Chafetz Chaim. Every year one irreligious Jew used to give a significant amount of charity to Rabbi Elya Lapian's *yeshivah*. Once, Rabbi Elya approached the man and asked him why he would donate so much money to the *yeshivah*. The man replied with a remarkable story:

When I was a boy, I desired to try to see what the *yeshivah* experience was like. So I applied to the Chafetz Chaim's Yeshiva in Radin. Unfortunately I didn't do well on the entrance exam, so I didn't get into the Yeshiva. My train wasn't leaving till the next morning so I had nowhere to sleep. Sheepishly, I knocked on the Chafetz Chaim's door and asked him if I could sleep that night in the Yeshiva. The Chafetz Chaim told me unfortunately there was limited space at the Yeshiva so I couldn't stay there. However, he added, it would be an honor for him if I stayed by him for the night. I graciously accepted the invitation. It was a cold winter night, and I had difficulty sleeping with the thin blanket the Chafetz Chaim provided me with. In the middle of the night, the door opened. There stood the saintly figure of the Chafetz Chaim. He took off his coat, kneelled beside me, and gently put the coat over me. I slept the rest of the night soundly. I will always remember that extraordinary act of kindness. It is for this reason that every year I donate money to Yeshiva. I still feel the warmth of the Chafetz Chaim's coat on me."

Giving in Our Own Personal Lives

As a physical therapist that has been privileged to help many people with disabilities and injuries, I have experienced firsthand what it means to give to another human being. One story stands out in my own mind from my years as a therapist, and it occurred when I was interning at a unit for spinal cord injury.

Anthony was a middle aged man with an injury which resulted in a rare condition called central cord syndrome. His legs were nearly normal, but his arms were almost completely paralyzed. He had some movement in his fingers and elbows, but that was about it. When I first began working with Anthony, he was full of rage about his condition and would often scream at me to leave him alone. As time wore on, however, he softened and apologized for his earlier behavior. The two of us eventually became good friends. As I worked with him, he began opening up to me about his life, and sharing his experiences he had a young child. He told me about when he first opened a flower shop that would later become a booming business. We shared a lot together during those months of rehabilitation.

The time came for Anthony and me to say good-bye. His friend told me that Anthony wanted to see me in his room. When I went into his room, I found him sitting in a chair with tears spilling softly down his cheeks. He told me how much he felt I helped him, not only physically but emotionally as well. He had told his friend to buy me a key chain with gold lettering in a Judaica bookstore for me. But what made a much more lasting impression on me was that he wrote me a goodbye card. He wrote the card with the help of his occupational therapist and it took hours for him to do. I held the card in my hands as I read the shaky handwriting. The card read, "Israel, a token to say thanks and a symbol for all the help you will unlock. Sincerely, your patient and friend, Anthony." I have kept this card in my room for many years now, and it continues to give me strength, and teach me what the power of giving can do.

Spiritual Exercises

1. Try to remember a time in your life when you did a selfless act. How did you feel at the time of the act? How did you feel afterwards? Why do you suppose you felt this way?

2. Try to remember a time in your life when you did a selfish act. How did you feel at the time? How did you feel afterwards? Why do you suppose you felt this way?

3. Try to think of one small act you can do each day to give to someone else or to an institution, either physically, emotionally, spiritually, or financially. Try to make sure you perform this act before you go to sleep at night. Then try to monitor how it changes your day.

4. Try to think of one role model, either a famous personality, or someone in your personal life who is a selfless giver. Try to concentrate on their face for a few moments each day. Try to think of ways you can emulate that person.

Afterword
Yearning for Godliness

My Heart is filled with yearning
For the higher vistas of the spirit.
Give me the Light of God,
The pleasure and the delight
Of the living God.
The privilege of standing in the palace
Of the King of the universe.
I always aspire for the God of my father,
My whole heart is devoted to His love,
My awe of Him exalts me.
I hope for deliverance and light,
For the dawn of knowledge and illumination.
I will find delight
In the goodness of the Lord,
In contemplating the vastness of His hiding place,
In his supernal might.

~ Rabbi Abraham Isaac Kook

THANK YOU FOR COMING ALONG with me on my journey. I hope I have helped you deepen your relationship to God. Always remember that life is a continuous journey, it doesn't end with my book. We are all still travelers, looking for lampposts on our way to illuminate our path.

The person that we are today is forever changing. It is not where we are now; it is where we are yearning to be. The sixth Lubavitcher Rebbe was once looking out the window during *cheder* (Jewish class). His teacher said to him "Always remember, Yosef Yitzchak, it is better to be on the outside looking in, then on the inside looking out." This is a very deep idea. Someone who is on the *outside* looking *into* the classroom wishing he was in the class studying Torah is at that moment much closer to God than someone *inside* the class yearning to be *outside* the Torah class.

This idea is true in many areas. Someone living in Israel but is always dreaming to come and live in America is still farther from Israel than someone living in America who dreams all day of someday coming to live in Israel. We are what we are yearning for. What we yearn for makes all of the difference in the world.

Living Inspired

I began this book writing about the importance of finding meaning in the *mitzvot* as a way to enhance our Judaism. It is now time to come around full circle and continue this theme. We all know that there are moments in our lives when we feel powerful, inspired, and close to God. What are we to do with those moments?

The Torah answers this question. When discussing donating money to the Temple it is written in the verse "All of whose hearts feel, should bring their money or vessels to the Temple." The emphasis of this verse is translating inspiration into action, from *feeling* into *doing. Carpe diem*, it is about seizing the moment and not allowing it to pass. For we are taught in *Pirkei Avot* that it is *action,* not *study* that yields the greatest results. We have studied much of the beauty and depth of Judaism, the time has come to translate those ideas into our day to day actions, and begin to yearn for Godliness.

The Hidden Path

We live in a world where many of us look at Judaism as a mere system of laws, as a religion that is dry, rigid, and cold. Few of us have experienced Judaism as something passionate, beautiful, and meaningful. Many people think of *halachah* as a strict set of rules that must be performed as one performs a chore.

This is why Rebbe Nachman of Breslov says that we must turn the *halachot* that we learn into prayers. What does this mean? One can study the complex laws of lighting the candles of Shabbat and leave it at that. Or one can begin by praying to God, "Please let the light of Shabbat enter my life on Shabbat, please let it radiate and illuminate my soul, please let me do it properly so that for one moment there is no wall between the Master of the World and me. Please allow my intentions to be pure when I light so that my Shabbat should be peaceful and pure."

A Paradigm Shift

One can either say that there are 613 restrictive *mitzvot* or that there are 613 ways to get closer to God. We live in a world with so much temptation and materialism, the *only* way Judaism can remain meaningful is if we take this approach. Furthermore, the Sages of the Talmud expound the very first word of the Ten Commandments, *Anochi Hashem,* "I am God." The word *anochi* stands for *ana nafshi ketavit yehavit,* "I wrote it Myself and gave it." This means God so to speak gave a part of Himself into each commandment. When we partake in a *mitzvah* we are connecting with a piece of the Divine.

In Judaism, the experience really *precedes* the laws; the laws are merely an outgrowth of what we as a People feel. This approach suddenly turns Judaism into a faith laden with infinite beauty; one only needs to explore to uncover its depth. It is written in Psalms, "Taste and see that God is good." First one must *taste*, one must *experience*, before he or she can see that God is good.

The Talmud talks about what a *mitzvah* can do. It is written in the verse, *va-asitem otam*, which means "and you shall do them," which refers to performing the *mitzvot*. However, the Talmud expounds these words exegetically. It writes that one can read these words as *va-asitem attem*, "and they shall do for you." This means it is the *mitzvot* that are *doing something to us,* namely elevating us into becoming better people. What a beautiful and radically different way of looking at the *mitzvot*, indeed!

The Soul of Man

Man is born with two opposing natures. He is born with a body, filled with temptations and lusts. He is born with a soul, yearning for something transcendent. It is written in the book of Proverbs, "The candle of God is the soul of man." Rabbi Shneur Zalman of Liadi explains this verse beautifully in the *Tanya*. A candle is composed of two parts: the body, which is made of the wax and wick, and the flame. The flame needs the body to survive, and yet the flame is always striving upward, away from the body. Moreover, the flame cannot be captured physically, it is constantly evolving moving. The ironic part is that the flame can only survive as the wax disintegrates. So too it is with our souls. It is constantly striving for more, reaching for Heaven, and yet it remains attached to the ground, and needs its body to survive in this world. However, it gains strength as the body is weakened. This means the less materialistic and base the body is, the stronger the soul becomes. When the body disintegrates completely with death, the soul too, just like the flame, dies, only it now goes to its rightful place in the World of Truth.

The Hidden Path

The Atheist and the Believer

What is the difference between the man of faith and the man of happenstance? A well known Yiddish proverb is, "The atheist has no answers, the believer has no questions." There is a kernel of truth to this maxim, albeit only a kernel. The atheist's life must be one of only despair and misery with a lifetime of unanswered questions. Why is there so much suffering in the world? Why do good righteous people endure such pain, while so many terrible people enjoy a life of ease and comfort? Is there no justice? And why should morality matter if there is no Higher Being to answer to? And if there is no Higher Being, why does one feel bad after doing something wrong? Where does that feeling come from? And is there really no Afterlife? A person withers away slowly with nothing to look forward to, but the grave! No Greater Place to reach, no place where justice can finally be extracted! No End of Days, no Messiah, just a world of chaos, war, and struggles! Furthermore, do our actions really have no meaning? What a dark and depressing world the atheist resides in.

The believer certainly does not have all the answers, but at least he has the *beginning* of the answers. Furthermore, he has the solace of knowing that at least there *are* answers. There is a Higher Being who will one day teach us what it all means. We are just a spec in the cosmos, and the Infinite Power has reasons that right now be cannot understand, but one day we will. Yes, our actions *do* have meaning. Yes, evil people will one day have their day of reckoning. Yes, there is a better Place awaiting us after the grave. Yes, there will be a great Day when there will be true peace in the world.

It is for these reasons that I wrote this book. The life of faith, though not often the path most obvious to all, is the only way to find solace in this world. The lucky ones understand this intuitively. Others stumble upon the path accidentally, by finding a good book that connects them to who they truly are. The unlucky ones endure suffering before they come to discover this truth.

Everyone at some point in their lives feels an unexplained sense of longing and emptiness. This feeling is not solved by the material benefits of this world. On the contrary, it only adds to the longing. Some people sadly enough continue to immerse themselves in materialistic pursuits with the vain hope that it will fulfill this void. However, if a person will be brutally honest, the void only continues to grow bigger. What creates this void? How does one get rid of it? What are the answers?

There is a remarkable parable which can answer these questions. Imagine a princess who was exiled and forced to live amongst commoners. As time goes by, the princess forgets what life was like in the palace. However, as much as she enjoys living with the common folk, she cannot escape the feeling that she once knew life has more to offer. She becomes acquainted with a young pauper. The pauper senses the young maiden's unhappiness. He is eager to please her and saves up some of his money to buy her fresh radishes. He presents it to her with a triumphant smile. She smiles thinly back, kindly thanking him for the present, but he senses that she is even more distraught. Frustrated the young pauper saves up even more money to but her fresh potatoes. Again, she has a similar reaction. This goes on for quite some time, never satisfying the young princess, for deep down she is used to the royalty and the finest cuisine.

So it is with the human condition. We are all princes and princesses, children of the living God. Our soul is used to royalty. It cannot be satisfied with mundane physical pleasures. It yearns for something much greater. This book is a quest to help us find what the soul craves for, to recover its lost royalty.

Our Choices Make Up Who We Are

In the Harry Potter saga, the wise sage and wizard Albus Dumbledore tells Harry "It is our choices, Harry, that show what we truly are, far more than our abilities." This idea is very much a Jewish idea. The Torah teaches us to "choose life," that is, to voluntarily *choose* to live a life of meaning.

Man lives in this world a short number of years. It is the choices that one makes that make the person who he or she is. Our fate is not chosen for us, it is we choose our destiny. Rabbi Soloveitchik once said, "Against your will you are born, and against your will you will die, but with your free will do you live. Man is born as an object, dies as an object but is within his capacity to live as a subject."

When we think of death, we all think of what awaits us at the end of our lives, when our bodies descend to the grave. However, there is another type of death which the Talmud writes about. The Talmud says, "even when the wicked are alive, they are called dead." What does this mean? Death according to our tradition is the separation between body and soul. This occurs not only at the end of one's life, but it occurs during sin as well. When a person sins, his or her body is distancing itself from its soul. It is separating itself from the Godly part inside of itself.

This also then explains the deep sense of joy and contentment one can feel when one does a *mitzvah* with proper intentions. A *mitzvah* is an act of piety which brings the body closer to God. His or her soul is now even more profoundly bound to its Source. This is a heightened feeling of living which cannot otherwise be explained. This is why the Talmud says that even when a righteous person dies, he or she is still alive. Their soul continues to thrive on the incredible life force it had been given in the *tzaddik's* lifetime.

Staying Connected

One of the miracles recorded in the Midrash concerning the first Holy Temple is that the *Lechem HaPanim* (Show Bread) never became stale. However, the Tzemach Tzedek points out that if we were to take this bread out of the Temple, the bread would turn into ordinary bread and become stale. This teaches us a fundamental rule in life; as long as one stays close to the Source, he or she will remain hot. This is our lifelong mission, to be as the Show Bread, always trying to stay close, feel inspired, and never grow stale.

This message is also found in the meaning of Passover. The holiday is themed after the importance of alacrity. Matzah must be baked with speed; it is time that will cause matzah to become *chametz* (leavened). This is because at the moment of the Exodus, the Jewish People were at the pinnacle of their faith. They could not delay leaving Egypt, they had to leave at *that moment*, a little bit longer and they would have remained enslaved, if not physically than emotionally. Their faith would have become stale; the moment of inspiration would have been lost forever. And so on Passover we commemorate the redemption by remembering the zeal of our ancestors. Sitting at the Passover *Seder*, we are not just remembering, we are *reliving.* For redemption to occur, we must seize the moment. We bake the dough quickly, as our ancestors did in preparing to leave Egypt, not allowing the dough to rise. It is by no coincidence, the Talmud says, that the words *matzah* and *mitzvah* are very similar. It again stresses the importance of fulfilling God's commandments with zeal and enthusiasm. We have all experienced at some point the consequences of waiting too long to do something important. When we finally decide to do it, it is too late and the opportunity has slipped away.

Taking Action

There is a disturbing Midrash in Genesis concerning the Sacrifice of Isaac. In Genesis we find that Abraham surpassed the last of the ten trials; he decided to go against his own trait of mercy and compassion to obey the word of God. God asked him to sacrifice his beloved son Isaac and Abraham agreed. After traveling to the designated spot on the mountain for the sacrifice, Abraham bound Isaac to the Altar. He raised the knife to snuff out the life he had wanted so desperately to bring into the world. At the last moment, the Angel Gabriel came and stopped him. The Angel told him that this was all a test to see if Abraham had full trust in God and was willing to obey His every word.

This portion of the story is all recorded in Genesis. But here is where the Midrash continues. After the Angel came and stopped Abraham, Abraham begged to cut Isaac, at least a little bit. The angel replied no. Still Abraham pleaded to shed at least one drop.

How are we to understand this Midrash? Abraham, our compassionate father known for his abounding kindness, who pleaded with God to spare the wicked city of Sodom, who left every side of his tent open to guests, suddenly became bloodthirsty? After being told that this was a test, shouldn't he have breathed a big sigh of relief and taken off Isaac from the Altar and returned home? Wouldn't that be the Abraham we all know and love? And yet we find Abraham begging to at least spill one drop from his own beloved son!

The Midrash is teaching us a profound lesson. At the moment that Abraham raised the knife, he had reached his ultimate potential. He had demonstrated his total trust in God and his willingness to obey His word at all costs. At that moment, he was completely one with God. The winds of Judaism began to blow, as his people were born from this act. Every year we blow the *shofar,* the ram's horn, on Rosh Hashanah to remind God of the ram that Abraham offered in Isaac's stead.

What did Abraham at that moment want to do? He wanted to at least do something *physical,* something tangible, to make his intentions more real. He wanted to show God that he really truly was willing to sacrifice Isaac. He knew how powerful this moment was, he knew this moment would be forever part of the Jewish consciousness. So he sought to make it even more real, to take a physical action and at least spill one drop of Isaac's blood. It is no coincidence that the Sages say Abraham is compared to the holiday of Passover. Abraham, whose whole life was about running to do the will of God. The verse says that the morning he was to sacrifice Isaac, "Abraham arose early in the morning." He ran to serve the three strangers who appeared at his tent, and treated them as distinguished guests.

This was a powerful lesson indeed. The importance of solidifying our thoughts into actions, of taking a moment of inspiration and transforming it into something we can see and feel. Judaism is about making our thoughts count. This is the message I want to leave everyone in this book. Each and every one of us feels at some point a yearning to get close to God. The point of these moments is to right away convert these intentions into deeds. By this, we are drawing from the higher world and bringing it into the lower world.

We find the idea again by the reunion between Joseph and his father Jacob. Jacob was tormented for years by Joseph's disappearance. Jacob was forced to believe the worst; that his beloved son was torn to pieces by a wild animal as Joseph's brothers asserted. One can only imagine the feeling Jacob had when he learned that not only was Joseph alive and well, but he was the viceroy to Egypt, the most powerful country in the world at the time! Finally the moment arrived when Joseph went to see his father. He arrived with an entourage of servants in an elegant carriage. The Torah writes that Jacob delayed seeing his son for a moment. Rashi explains that Jacob was reciting the *Shema*, the fundamental prayer we recite daily when we acknowledge the yoke of Heaven and the importance of the *mitzvot*. Why? Why did ho choose *that* moment to fulfill this mitzvah? Couldn't he have waited to fulfill it later; after all, he hadn't seen his son in over twenty years? Did reciting the daily prayer of *Shema* take precedence over arguably the most important event in his life?

The answer again is this same idea. True, Jacob could have waited until after he became reunited with his son to recite the *Shema*. However, he knew the powerful feeling of inspiration he was experiencing at the moment he saw Joseph, a feeling of joy quite like nothing he had ever experienced before. It was at this moment he *knew*, with certainty, what he must do. *Carpe diem*, he must seize the moment. He must challenge this feeling quickly into a *physical act*, into a *mitzvah*, into a prayer. This prayer, with such a spiritual charge would be perhaps the greatest payer Jacob would ever recite. What a connection he must have experienced at that moment to the Divine.

Rabbi Shneur Zalman of Liadi once said to think of the 613 commandments in the Torah as 613 rays of light coming from the One Above. When we perform a *mitzvah*, we are connecting to its Source, the One who created us. What an evocative idea, and what an innovative way to look at *mitzvot*. A *mitzvah* then is not a burden, but rather an opportunity. This is the hidden path which our ancestors have taught us. We are fortunate that we don't really need to begin searching for God on our own, since we have already been given a path handed down to us throughout the centuries by our parents and grandparents.

Following the Footsteps

I would like to relate one of my favorite stories from Rebbetzin Esther Jungreis. She tells the story of when she was a little girl and was once walking with her grandfather in the snow. Her grandfather told her to follow his lead and jump into his footprints. Afterward he asked her if she understood the message. She nodded her head, even though at the time she did not understand the message. Only years later did she fully understand the message her grandfather was trying to impart. There are many snowstorms in our lives. The piles of snow can run very deep. It is so easy to fall, to stumble, and to lose our way. But before us, our ancestors have given us a path. The path goes all the way back to our father Abraham and our mother Sarah. We can follow their footsteps in the snow, knowing that we will be safe, even when they are no longer there to guide our way. Even when we fall, we can look for the next footprint in the snow toward our destination.

I was once at a *berit* (ritual circumcision) when the *mohel* (the person who performs the ritual) arose to speak just a few minutes before the circumcision. He relayed a powerful idea from the famous French artist Pierre-August Renoir. Renoir had terrible arthritis at the end of his life. It pained him so much to paint that he used to attach the brushes to his forearm and apply bigger strokes on a bigger canvas. Claude Monet, Renoir's contemporary, would watch as his teacher grimaced in pain and continued to paint. One day Monet approached him, "Why do you continue to paint if it means you have to endure such great agony? You have already produced many fine pieces of art. Why not retire?"

Renoir responded, "The pain that I feel is only temporary, but my paintings will live on for all future generations to appreciate and feel inspired."

The *mohel* continued and explained that so it is with the infant who undergoes the circumcision. The pain the baby will feel is only temporary, but the act of circumcision is linking him all the way to our father Abraham, and insuring the continuity of the Jewish people for the future. The baby has joined the eternal covenant.

And so it is with all of the *mitzvot*. Every deed we perform matters significantly. Our actions *do* matter. God shows His love for us by caring about all of our actions throughout the day. For we all know the greatest sign of love is when we care about what our loved one is doing throughout the day and throughout their lives. At times we feel inadequate, little more than a speck of dust in a vast unending universe. But at times we feel something deep within us telling us that somehow we *do* mean something, that the choices we make do make a difference. Every one of us has special talents and skills, gifts that were either given to us at birth or acquired during our lifetime. Utilizing our gifts and how we choose to utilize them is what makes us into who we are. The choice for smallness or greatness lies within all of us. It is my hope and prayer that all of us use our gifts to help build the world into a better home for ourselves and our children and bring ourselves and those around us closer to our Creator above.

Let me end this afterword on yearning for Godliness with the same brief prayer which we began with, from the song "Beloved of Your Soul" by Rabbi Eliezer Azikiri:

Please be revealed and spread upon me, my Beloved, the shelter of Your peace. Illuminate the world with Your Glory that we may rejoice and be glad with You. Hasten, show us love, for the time has come, and show us grace as in the days of old.

With Love,

Yisroel

Appendix:
Biographies

Aaron, Rabbi David. Founder of *Isralight* (1986) and author of the best-selling *Endless Light, Seeing God*, and *Love is My Religion*.

Alter of Slobodka. One of the great leaders of the *Mussar* Movement in Eastern Europe, and long time leader of the *yeshivah* in Slobodka, Lithuania.

Ari. Rabbi Isaac Luria, a prominent sixteenth-century mystic and Kabbalistic, whose teachings advanced the study of Kabbalah and influenced Chassidut.

Baal Shem Tov. Rabbi Israel ben Eliezer, eighteenth-century founder of Chassidut. He experienced a spiritual enlightenment while secluded in the Carpathian Mountains, and taught a doctrine of ecstatic mysticism.

Bachya ben Asher, Rabbi. A medieval author who is one of the first writers to incorporate Jewish mysticism into his commentary on the Torah.

Carlebach, Rabbi Shlomo. A composer of popular Jewish melodies, many of which have been incorporated into the Jewish prayer service.

Chafetz Chaim. Rabbi Israel Meir Kagan is best known for his *Mishnah Berurah*, a thorough and influential commentary on *Shulchan Aruch, Orach Chaim*, as well as some other works, include one on the evils caused by slander.

Eliach, Yaffa Historian of the Jewish People, especially during Nazi Germany, and author of *Hasidic Tales of the Holocaust*, among other works.

Freedman, Rav Binny. Educational Director of Isralight and decorated veteran of the Israel Defense Forces.

Gaon of Vilna. Rabbi Elijah ben Solomon Zalman, an eighteenth-century author and Kabbalist who criticized the Chassidic movement for its laxity of Torah study, excessive reverence for its leaders, and doctrines on the nature of God.

Heschel, Abraham Joshua. A direct descendant of the great Chassidic master the Aptar Rav, he received rabbinic ordination, and espoused Conservative Judaism but remained observant in a traditional sense.

Hirsch, Rabbi Samson Raphael. A nineteenth-century German rabbi who developed the teaching *Torah im Derech Eretz*, he also wrote a commentary on the Pentateuch, Psalms, and other works, and devoted much time to refuting the nascent Reform movement.

Jungreis, Rebbetzin Esther. Founder of Hineni organization, and a Holocaust survivor, she has authored *The Committed Life* along with many other titles.

Kaplan, Rabbi Aryeh. Highly trained in physics and mysticism, and prolific writer whose works incorporate traditional Jewish rationalism, mysticism, and science. Although many of his writings were distributed to high-schoolers, they offer depth for even the most intellectual of adults.

Kook, Rabbi Abraham Isaac. The first chief rabbi of then-Palestine, now Israel, he wrote extensively on Jewish mysticism, aesthetics, and one of the early proponents of a religious Zionist movement.

Kotzker Rebbe. A nineteenth-century Chassidic rabbi who devoted his life to teaching about personal analysis and introspection. He burned all of his writings before his death, but his teachings and stories live on in an oral tradition.

Levi Yitzchak of Berditchev, Rabbi. One of the main students of the Maggid of Mezeritch, he was famous for interpreting people's actions positively, and also wrote *Kedushat Levi*, a multi-volume commentary on the Torah.

Luzzatto, Rabbi Moshe Chaim. Best known for his *Mesillat Yesharim* ("The Path of the Just"), an eighteenth-century work on character development which contains Kabbalistic principles although he never uses mystical terms, he wrote secular plays as well.

Maimonides, Rabbi Moses. Medieval rationalist, author of the *halachic* work *Mishneh Torah*, one of the cornerstones of Jewish law, and the *Guide to the Perplexed*, which synthesized traditional Judaism with Aristotelian philosophy.

Moshe Leib Sossover, Rabbi. A third-generation Chassidic spent much time redeeming Jews from captivity, since it was common for the authorities to kidnap Jews for ransom.

Nachman of Breslov, Rabbi. A great-grandson of the Baal Shem Tov, he developed his spirituality with a strict regimen of prayer, asceticism, and self-affliction. Although he suffered from sadness much of his life, he devoted many of his teachings to the importance of happiness.

Rashi. Rabbi Solomon ben Isaac, an eleventh-century French rabbi and teacher, prolific scholar and commentator on the Hebrew Bible, Talmud, his works are of primary significance for proper understanding of traditional Jewish teachings.

Shafier Rabbi Binyamin. Founder of the popular website theshmuz.com, he offers insightful advice on daily concerns shared by all, and has developed these talks into a series of books.

Shapira, Rabbi Klonymous Kalman. The Piaseczner Rebbe, a leader of European Jewry during the Second World War, and author of *Chovat HaTalmidim*, "The Obligation of the Students," and *Aish Kodesh*, "Holy Fire," a work compiled in the Warsaw Ghetto.

Shneur Zalman of Liadi, Rabbi. The founder of Chabad Chassidut, and student of the Maggid of Mezeritch, he authored a commentary on *Shulchan Aruch*, but is well known for the *Tanya*, a blend of the mystical and intellectual teachings that Chabad Chassidim study daily.

Soloveitchik, Rabbi Joseph B. A twentieth-century rabbi who received rabbinic ordination in Europe and a Ph.D. in Jewish philosophy, he moved to America in the 1930's, and he revitalized Yeshiva University in New York City, where many of his students became prominent rabbis in their own right, and developed a Jewish philosophy that merged rationalism and mysticism.

Spira, Rabbi Yisroel. A member of the Bluzhiver dynasty, he was a Holocaust survivor, but his wife and children were murdered during the war, and he later moved to Brooklyn and then Israel.

Tzadok of Lublin, Rabbi. An eighteenth-century rabbi and author who devoted the first part of his life to studying "revealed texts" like the Talmud, and then devoted the rest of his life to studying and commenting on the esoteric Jewish writings.

Weinberger, Rabbi Moshe. The Rabbi of Congregation Aish Kodesh in Woodmere, Rabbi Weinberger is a prominent lecturer in the Chassidic community.

Vital, Rabbi Chaim. A sixteenth/seventeenth-century mystic who studied with many of the prominent Kabbalists in Safed, and author of *Etz Chaim*, one of the principle works on Kabbalah.

Weinberg, Rabbi Yechiel Yaakov. He combined a deep understanding of *halachah* with the Slobodka *Mussar* movement. He also received a Ph.D. for a thesis on the masoretic text.

23572188R00151

Made in the USA
Charleston, SC
28 October 2013